Instructor's Manual to Accompany About Professional Baking

GAIL SOKOL

Printed in the United States of America
2 3 4 5 XXX 09 08 07 06

For more information contact Thomson Delmar Learning,
5 Maxwell Drive, Clifton Park, NY 12065.

Or find us on the World Wide Web at http://www.delmarlearning.com

Library of Congress Catalog Card Number: ISBN 1-4018-4922-9
ISBN-10: 1-4018-4923-7 / ISBN-13: 978-1-4018-4923-8

Contents

Preface

It is with great pleasure that I present you with this textbook. As a baking instructor, I have had many proficient students capable of carrying out a recipe to its successful conclusion. Yet very few students understand the science behind the scenes.

Many years ago, some of the world's most famous bakers and pastry chefs learned by doing and working through apprenticeships under a skilled master baker. Repetitive skills, guided by the master, were the sole teaching tool. Today's bakers, due to a global society, deal with ever-changing trends and a fusion of techniques from around the world.

Baking is an art as well as a science. To bake well, it is necessary to give students an appreciation of the interactions that occur between the various ingredients through chemical reactions and basic scientific principles.

The various baking principles and techniques in this text lay a foundation from which students can learn. Some basic principles of science are taught as an explanation as to why ingredients, combined in specific ways, form baked goods that are consistent every time they are prepared. The chapters focus on ingredients, how they relate to baking techniques and principles, and how they interact among each other.

Each chapter culminates in recipes that represent specific principles that were taught within the chapter with a section before each recipe demonstrating the lessons the recipe teaches from the principles within the chapter. This *Instructor's Manual* should serve as an outline. Each chapter of the guide has an introduction from which a chapter outline follows.

The Answers to the Review Questions follow the chapter outline. A group of test questions have been provided along with answers to make test preparation easier.

Gail D. Sokol, C. C.

SUPPLEMENTS

Student Workbook

ISBN: 1418019720

This *Student Workbook* is a comprehensive assessment tool that reinforces the content of the text.
Included are additional student activities and study questions.

Electronic Classroom Manager (ECM)

The *Electronic Classroom Manager* is a CD-ROM containing all of the instructor resources available to accompany the *About Professional Baking* text. This valuable resource simplifies the planning and implementation of the instructional program. Included in the ECM are chapter-specific PowerPoint presentations, a computerized test bank, and additional lesson plans.

Online Companion

The *Online Companion,* located at http://www.culinary.delmar.com, provides students and instructors additional resources to accompany the *About Professional Baking* text and curriculum.

Included in the Student *Online Companion* are URLs to culinary Web sites. In addition, there is a password protected component of this Web site. The student access code is sealed in an envelope in the back of their textbook. The password protected resources include:

e-Video Clips: Professionally produced video clips highlight essential baking techniques for students. These ideal study aids are available online at no cost with a unique access code that is provided with each new textbook.

Recipes in Electronic Format: An electronic file with all *About Professional Baking* recipes is provided in a format that makes it easy to import into popular recipe and chef software. A unique access code is provided with each new textbook for online access.

Included in the Instructor *Online Companion* are additional activities and answers, lesson plans, PowerPoint® presentations, and the e-Videos and recipes that are also on the Student *Online Companion.* For access to these materials, visit the Instructor Center at http://www.culinary.delmar.com.

Please note: The access code packaged within the back of your text only allows users access to the e-Video Clips and recipe database for 16 weeks from the initial log-in. This same content is available for unlimited use in the "Instructor Center" of the Culinary Web site (http://www.culinary.delmar.com).

About Professional Baking DVD Series

ISBN: 141801348X

The *About Professional Baking DVD Series* contains 4 hours of all new video footage available on three DVDs. Hosted by Chef Gail Sokol, the step-by-step instruction emphasizes the science and technique involved with baking. A correlation guide to align the content of the DVDs to the text is packaged with the series.

Additional Culinary Arts titles available from Thomson Delmar Learning

Delmar/About Professional Baking DVD Series, ISBN 1-4180-1348-X.

Henderson/About Wine, ISBN 1-4018-3711-5

Garlough/Modern Garde Manger, ISBN 1-4018-5009-X

For more information about these or any other culinary titles, please visit our Web site at www.culinary.delmar.com, or call 800-477-3692.

CHAPTER 1
Mise en Place

For video segments that correspond to this chapter, please see the About Professional Baking DVD series, Disk 1's chapter: *Mise en Place.*

Objectives

After reading this chapter, the student should be able to:

- ✓ Demonstrate organizational skills necessary to bake successfully.
- ✓ Demonstrate proper measurement of solids and liquids by volume.
- ✓ Demonstrate how to weigh ingredients on a baker's scale and a digital scale.

Key Terms

baker's percentages
calibrated
formulas
meniscus
mise en place
scaling
temperature danger zone

Chapter Outline

I. Introduction—The title of this chapter is Mise en Place, which translated from the French means "getting everything ready and in its place." The chapter emphasizes the importance of organization in order to achieve success when baking. Commonly used ingredients, tools, and pieces of equipment are discussed briefly to familiarize the student with these common terms.

II. Organizational Skills Needed for Baking
  - A. Reading the Recipe Carefully
  - B. Identifying Tools and/or Equipment Needed
  - C. Gathering All Necessary Ingredients, Tools, and Equipment Close to the Work Area
  - D. Preparing the Pans
  - E. Measuring Properly
  - F. Practicing Good Sanitation
  - G. Handling Eggs

III. How to Measure the Ingredients in this Book

IV. The Correct Tools of Measurement
  - A. Volume Measurement
    - 1. Properly Measuring a Liquid by Volume
    - 2. Properly Measuring a Solid by Volume

V. How to Use a Baker's Scale
  - A. Problems with a Baker's Scale
    - 1. Example: Using a Baker's Scale

VI. How to Use a Digital Scale
  - A. Problems with a Digital Scale

VII. Baker's Percentages

VIII. Baking Tools and Equipment Defined
  - A. Baguette Pan
  - B. Bain Marie
  - C. Baker's Peel
  - D. Banneton
  - E. Bench Scraper
  - F. Bowl Scraper
  - G. Coupler
  - H. Double Boiler
  - I. Electric Mixer
  - J. False-Bottom Tart Pan
  - K. Grater
  - L. Loaf Pan
  - M. Metal Cake Ring
  - N. Microplane Zester
  - O. Muffin Tin
  - P. Offset Spatula
  - Q. Parchment Paper
  - R. Pastry Bag
  - S. Pastry Brush
  - T. Pastry Tip
  - U. Popover Pan
  - V. Ramekin
  - W. Sheet Pans
  - X. Sieve or Strainer
  - Y. Sifter
  - Z. Silicone Baking Mats
  - AA. Silicone Baking Pan
  - BB. Springform Pan
  - CC. Squirt Bottle
  - DD. Tube Pan
  - EE. Zester

IX. Helpful Hints in Using This Text

X. Procedure to Make Parchment Cake Pan Liners for Round Cake Pans

XI. How to Line Sheet Pans with Parchment Paper

XII. Proper Preparation of Cake Pans before Baking
   A. Seven Steps to Follow to Ensure a Cake's Removal
      1. Before Baking
      2. After Baking
XIII. Preparing Muffin Tins
XIV. Forming a Parchment Cone
XV. Sifting Dry Ingredients
   A. Sifting and Measuring by Weight
   B. Sifting and Measuring by Volume
XVI. Storing Baked Goods
XVII. Properly Wrapping Baked Goods to Be Frozen

Note to Instructors: A list of exercises are included as teaching tools to be used before the act of baking actually begins.

- ✓ It would benefit a beginning student to weigh various solid and liquid ingredients on a baker's scale and/or digital scale for practice.
- ✓ Reading a sample of recipes out loud along with the procedure would also benefit the beginning student as an exercise in learning. The instructor can identify tools, equipment, and unusual ingredients that will be needed.
- ✓ An emphasis on visualizing the steps to each procedure of the recipe being prepared is an excellent exercise, which the student will ultimately be doing on his or her own.
- ✓ Showing the student the various pieces of equipment and tools available in the kitchen before labs begin makes an excellent introductory lesson. Discussion should be encouraged as to how each piece of equipment or tool is used.
- ✓ A review of various measurements and conversions by both volume and weight, such as 4 fluid ounces = 1/2 cup, 3 teaspoons = 1 tablespoon, and so forth, should be emphasized and practiced.

Review Questions and Answers

1. **Why is it important to read a recipe carefully before you prepare it?**
   Proper understanding of what ingredients, tools, and equipment is needed for the recipe is crucial to its success. The mixing methods described in the recipe must be understood in order to successfully prepare it. Reading the recipe while making a mental image of what each stage should look like is an excellent way to promote a thorough understanding.
2. **Can a thin liquid like water be weighed on a baker's scale?**
   Yes. One fluid ounce of water is only slightly different from 1 dry ounce of water. However, for other liquids, a dry ounce does not equal a fluid ounce. The one exception is water.
3. **What is the French phrase that means to "put everything in its place"?**
   Mise en place.
4. **Dry ingredients should not be packed when measuring them in a solid measuring cup. Name one ingredient that requires packing to get an accurate measure.**
   Brown sugar.
5. **What types of ingredients can be measured in a liquid volume measuring cup? What types of ingredients can be measured in solid measuring cups?**
   Liquids such as milk, juice, water, oil, and other ingredients listed in a recipe as fluid ounce measurements. Solid dry ingredients such as flour, sugar, cornstarch, and cocoa powder that are listed in a recipe in cups.
6. **Should 3 ounces of buttermilk be measured in a volume measuring cup or weighed on a scale? How about 4 fluid ounces of oil?**
   It is important to measure the ingredient the way it was written in the recipe. So, 3 ounces of buttermilk should be weighed on a scale since ounces is a weight measure, but 3 fluid ounces would be measured in a liquid volume measuring cup. Four fluid ounces of oil would be measured in a liquid measuring cup since it is written as a fluid ounce or volume measurement.
7. **What is the temperature danger zone and why is it so important?**
   The temperature danger zone is a temperature interval in which microorganisms thrive. It is between 41°F (5°C) and 135°F (57°C). (This interval may vary from state to state.) It is important to not allow foods to remain in the temperature danger zone for more than 4 hours. If a food is allowed to remain in the temperature danger zone, microorganisms will multiply exponentially, which increases the chances of foodborne illness.
8. **What is staling and how can it be slowed down?**
   Staling occurs when baked goods lose moisture over time due to evaporation into the air. Actual changes in the molecular structure of the starches within baked goods also occur over time, causing starch retrogradation or chemical staling. This is when the starches within the baked good bond more closely together over time going back to the state they were in before baking. Staling causes changes in a baked good's texture resulting in a dried out product with a flat, off taste.

Test Questions

MULTIPLE CHOICE

1. Why must students read a recipe carefully before beginning to bake?
   A. To identify the mixing method used
   B. To identify the necessary ingredients, tools, and equipment that are needed
   C. To envision what each stage of the recipe should look like
   D. All of the above
2. What is the term bakers use for the weighing of ingredients?
   A. Rounding
   B. Weighing
   C. Scaling
   D. Meniscus
3. What is the temperature danger zone?
   A. The temperature interval where microorganisms can multiply very rapidly
   B. The temperature interval where viruses can be spread from a cutting board to a food
   C. The temperature interval between 43°F (6°C) and 150°F (65°C)
   D. None of the above
4. What ingredient can you measure where a fluid ounce is equal to a dry ounce?
   A. When you are measuring molasses
   B. When you are measuring oil
   C. A and B
   D. When you are measuring water
5. When using baker's percentages to express a recipe or formula, what central ingredient is equated to 100 percent?
   A. Sugar
   B. Flour
   C. Eggs
   D. Baking powder
6. A woven basket made of coiled reed or willow that is floured and used to give rustic and hearth-type yeast doughs an attractive pattern is known as a:
   A. Bread dough basket
   B. Coupler
   C. Couche
   D. Banneton
7. Why is it not recommended to store baked goods in the refrigerator?
   A. They will get too cold.
   B. They will absorb unwanted odors from other foods.
   C. Refrigeration hastens starch retrogradation.
   D. Fillings in baked goods could thin down.
8. Which type of baked good is more likely to become stale?
   A. French bread
   B. Danish pastry
   C. Rich coffee cakes
   D. Doughnuts
9. Large quantities of these ingredients can help slow down staling in baked goods. What are they?
   A. Sugar
   B. Butter and other types of fat
   C. Baking soda
   D. A and B
10. What happens to baked goods during starch retrogradation?
    A. The starches within the baked good get closer together, much as they were before baking. They begin to recrystallize and develop a dry texture.
    B. The baked goods become frozen.
    C. Flavors in the baked good intensify.
    D. The starches break down, causing water to seep out.
11. What is the proper way to wrap baked goods that are to be frozen?
    A. The baked good should be frozen on a sheet pan for 1 day and then wrapped in aluminum foil.
    B. The baked good should be wrapped while it is still warm to maintain freshness.
    C. The cooled baked good should be wrapped airtight in plastic, then wrapped again in aluminum foil. It should then be placed in a plastic bag and secured tightly.
    D. The baked good should be placed in a paper bag and sealed tightly with tape.

TRUE OR FALSE

12. _____ An offset spatula is known as a banneton.
13. _____ In general, cakes should be removed from pans while they are hot.
14. _____ Volume measurements are equal to weight measurements.
15. _____ If a recipe calls for 4 fluid ounces of milk, it should be measured in a fluid ounce measuring cup, a volume measurement.

16. _____ If a recipe calls for 6 ounces of flour, it can be accurately measured in a solid measuring cup.

17. _____ After weighing sugar on a digital scale, other ingredients can successfully be weighed without removing the sugar first.

18. _____ Tube pans can be used for sponge cakes, angel food cakes, and pound cakes.

19. _____ Pastry bags are used to store flour and other dry ingredients.

20. _____ Professional muffin pans can hold between 2 and 4 dozen muffins.

21. _____ One advantage to using baker's percentages is that ingredients can be added or changed without changing the percentage of other ingredients.

Measurement Questions

1. ¼ cup = _____ fluid ounce(s)
2. 8 ounces = _____ pound(s)
3. 48 ounces = _____ pound(s)
4. 2 pints = _____ fluid ounce(s)
5. 1 tablespoon = _____ teaspoon(s)
6. 12 teaspoons = _____ tablespoon(s)
7. ½ of 3 pounds, 2 ounces = _____ ounce(s) or _____ pound(s) _____ ounce(s)
8. 2 tablespoons = _____ fluid ounce(s)
9. 3 cups = _____ pint(s)
10. 3¼ pounds = _____ ounce(s)
11. ¼ of 3 pounds, 12 ounces = _____ ounce(s)
12. 1 gallon = _____ pint(s)
13. ¼ gallon = _____ cup(s)
14. A gallon is a unit of _____
15. An ounce is a unit of _____
16. An inch is a unit of _____
17. A gram is a unit of _____
18. A milliliter is a unit of _____
19. 1 cup = _____ teaspoon(s)
20. 1 gallon = _____ fluid ounce(s)
21. 1 quart = _____ cup(s)
22. ½ cup = _____ tablespoon(s)
23. 40 cups = _____ pint(s)
24. 87 ounces = _____ pounds _____ ounce(s)
25. 1 liter = _____ milliliter(s)
26. A centimeter is a unit of _____
27. A tablespoon is a unit of _____
28. A pound is a unit of _____
29. A millimeter is a unit of _____
30. A fluid ounce is a unit of _____

Problems Using Baker's Percentages

1. Using the following percentages for a bread formula, calculate the quantities of each ingredient given the weight of the flour:

Bread flour	1 pound, 5 ounces	100%
Raw wheat germ	_____________	10%
Instant active dry yeast	_____________	0.6%
Water	_____________	67%
Kosher salt	_____________	1.2%

2. Keeping the baker's percentages the same, increase the formula from the previous example from a total yield of 2.3 pounds to a total yield of 35 pounds.

CHAPTER 2
Ingredients

For video segments that correspond to this chapter, please see the About Professional Baking DVD series, Disk 1's chapter: *Ingredients.*

Objectives

After reading this chapter, the student should be able to:

✓ Define the function of each of the major ingredients used in the bakeshop.

✓ Describe how ingredients work together within recipes to produce a specific finished product.

Key Terms

dry ingredients

homogenization

pasteurization

plasticity

solid ingredients

ultrapasteurization

wet ingredients

Chapter Outline

I. Introduction—This chapter describes the various ingredients used in a bakeshop. Each ingredient carries out a specific role or job. For example, some ingredients help the baked good to rise in the oven while others add to the baked good's structure. The roles of individual ingredients will be discussed in greater detail throughout the various chapters of this text. Students are asked to visualize baking as a team sport. The recipe is a game plan with the various ingredients being members of the team. Each member (or ingredient) has a specific role to carry out. Ingredients work as a team to create a final product—the baked good.

II. Wheat Flour

III. Sugar

IV. Eggs

V. Starches

VI. Gelatins

VII. Fats

VIII. Fats in Solid Form
- A. Butter
- B. Lard
- C. Vegetable Shortening
- D. High-Ratio or Emulsified Shortening
- E. Margarine

IX. Liquid Fats
- A. Corn Oil
- B. Canola Oil
- C. Olive Oil

X. Storage of Fats

XI. Dairy Products
- A. Milk
- B. Fresh Whole Milk
- C. Heavy Cream
- D. Low-Fat Milk
- E. Skim Milk
- F. Sweetened Condensed Milk
- G. Evaporated Milk
- H. Evaporated Skim Milk
- I. Cream Cheese
- J. Mascarpone Cheese
- K. Ricotta Cheese
- L. Cultured Dairy Products
  1. Buttermilk
  2. Yogurt
  3. Sour Cream

XII. Spices
- A. Allspice
- B. Cinnamon
- C. Clove
- D. Ginger
- E. Nutmeg
- F. Saffron
- G. Vanilla

XIII. Processed Flavorings
- A. Flavor Emulsions
- B. Flavor Oils
- C. Artificial Flavorings
- D. Alcoholic Flavorings

XIV. Seeds

XV. Salt

XVI. Peanut Butter

XVII. Nuts

XVIII. Products Derived from Nuts
- A. Almond Paste
- B. Marzipan

- C. Praline
- D. Nut Flours
- E. Nut Butters
- F. Gianduja

XIX. Coconut
- A. Cream of Coconut

XX. Toasting Coconut and Nuts
- A. Coconut and Sliced or Chopped Nuts
- B. Whole Nuts

XXI. Fruits
- A. Fresh Fruits
- B. Dried Fruits
- C. Unusual Fruits
- D. Fresh Currants
    1. Litchis
    2. Persimmons
    3. Passion Fruit
    4. Pomegranates
    5. Prickly Pears
    6. Quince
    7. Rhubarb
    8. Star Fruit

Review Questions and Answers

1. **Which ingredient has the power to slow down fermentation and even kill yeast?**
   Salt.
2. **Which ingredients are used to depress the freezing point of water when making frozen desserts like ice creams and sorbets?**
   Salt is used in certain ice cream machines to depress the freezing point of water to create water that is below freezing but still liquid with which to freeze an ice cream base. Sugar is used in sorbets and other frozen desserts to depress the freezing point of water to prevent the dessert from freezing too hard.
3. **What roles do fats play in baking?**
   Fats provide flavor, tenderizing abilities, moistness, and richness, and act as aerators.
4. **Name three cultured dairy products that can be used in conjunction with baking soda to aid in the leavening of baked goods.**
   Buttermilk, yogurt, and sour cream.
5. **What is plasticity? Why is it relevant to baking with fats?**
   Plasticity is defined as the ability of a fat to hold its shape at room temperature but still have the ability to be molded. Different fats have different melting points and each has a different degree of plasticity. Depending on what the baker is preparing, the plasticity of the fat can produce different characteristics in the finished product. For example, how much flakiness a pie crust will have will depend upon how plastic the fat is. The higher the plasticity, the greater the flakiness.
6. **How does the fact that sugar can depress the freezing point of water affect frozen desserts such as sorbets?**
   Sugar prevents sorbets and other frozen desserts from getting too firm and icy because the sugar lowers the freezing point of water. This means the temperature of the water must get below the freezing point to freeze and become ice. So a frozen dessert base containing a certain amount of sugar will never freeze too hard or to a point where it cannot be scooped.
7. **What is gianduja?**
   Gianduja is the combination of chocolate and toasted hazelnuts finely ground to a paste. It can be used to flavor a variety of desserts such as cake, mousses, cookies, and confections.
8. **Name some nuts that are commonly used by bakers.**
   Some commonly used nuts favored by bakers include almonds, cashews, hazelnuts, macadamia nuts, walnuts, and pistachios.
9. **What functions does sugar play?**
   Sugar provides sweetness, acts as a tenderizer, creates caramelization giving color to baked goods, absorbs moisture from the air providing moistness, aids fats in absorbing air during the creaming process, stabilizes meringues and whipped cream, provides yeast with food, and caramelizes and recrystallizes to create confections, frostings, and sauces.

Test Questions

MULTIPLE CHOICE

1. Of all the ingredients used by the baker, which one is the most important?
   A. Eggs
   B. Salt
   C. Yeast
   D. Wheat flour

2. Which of the following is not a function of sugar?
   A. Provides sweetness
   B. Prevents water from freezing to a solid state
   C. Aids fats in absorbing air during creaming
   D. Gives strength and structure to breads

3. What is the term bakers use to describe the ability of a fat to hold its shape at room temperature but still have the ability to be molded?
   A. Plasticity
   B. Pasteurization
   C. Homogenization
   D. Calibration

4. Why is butter frequently chosen for baking over other fats?
   A. It contains no saturated fat and is healthier.
   B. It has a rich taste and good mouthfeel.
   C. It is a highly plastic fat.
   D. It has a high melting point and maintains its shape in the oven.

5. What is pasteurization?
   A. Pasteurization is when fats are melted and allowed to cool down.
   B. Pasteurization is a process by which dairy products are heated to a specific temperature 161°F (72°C) for a minimum of 15 seconds to kill bacteria and other microorganisms.
   C. Pasteurization is the process by which dairy products are heated to 280°F (138°C) to increase shelf life.
   D. Pasteurization is the process of forcing fresh milk through holes under pressure to break the globules of fat into small droplets.

6. Which one of these ingredients is known as a cultured dairy product?
   A. Skim milk
   B. Buttermilk
   C. Ricotta cheese
   D. Sweetened condensed milk

7. Characteristic flavors and aromas in baked goods can be attributed to what category of ingredients?
   A. Butter
   B. Spices
   C. Brown sugar
   D. None of the above

8. How can salt potentially kill yeast?
   A. The salt crystals interfere with how the yeast multiply.
   B. Yeast can die because salt can depress the freezing point of water.
   C. Yeast cannot be killed by salt.
   D. When yeast is placed in direct contact with salt, any moisture within the yeast cells can be drawn out through osmosis, causing the yeast cell to shrivel up and die.

9. How should whole and ground spices be stored?
   A. Spices should be kept in a cool, dry, dark place.
   B. Spices should be stored in a container of alcohol to prevent evaporation of essential oils.
   C. Spices should be wrapped in aluminum foil before being frozen.
   D. Spices can be frozen anywhere and withstand any climatic condition.

10. Vegetable shortenings have undergone a chemical process to help them to become solid and more shelf stable. What is this process called?
    A. Homogenization
    B. Ultrapasteurization
    C. Cultured
    D. Hydrogenation

TRUE OR FALSE

11. _____ Peanuts are not true nuts.

12. _____ Evaporated milk is sweetened milk that has been condensed by evaporating 60 percent of the water from it.

13. _____ Cream cheese is typically used in cheese cakes, cookies, pastry doughs, and pie crusts.

14. _____ Cinnamon originates from the inner bark of a pine tree.

15. _____The hard outer coating of the nutmeg seed is covered with a red, lace-like material that, when ground, is mace.

16. _____ Gianduja is a combination of almonds and chocolate ground to a paste.

17. _____ Cream of coconut is made from the liquid that rises to the top of the coconut milk, with sugar and thickening agents added.

18. ______ The leaves of the rhubarb plant are poisonous and should never be eaten.

19. ______ Ground spices lose their flavor quickly because the essential oils have more surface area from which to evaporate.

20. ______ European-style butter has more milk fat than American butter.

CHAPTER 3

Wheat Flour—The Essential Grain (and Other Flours)

For video segments that correspond to this chapter, please see the About Professional Baking DVD series, Disk 1's chapter: *Yeast Doughs.*

Objectives

After reading this chapter, the student should be able to:

- ✓ List the five stages of the milling process.
- ✓ Explain the importance of wheat flour to the baker.
- ✓ Define how proteins in wheat flour relate to gluten.
- ✓ Understand the difference between hard wheats and soft wheats.
- ✓ Understand when to use a low-protein flour.
- ✓ Understand when to use a high-protein flour.
- ✓ Explain how flour is treated after milling.
- ✓ Understand the importance of gluten in making yeast breads.
- ✓ Control gluten in baked goods without yeast.

Key Terms

all-purpose flour
bleaching
bread flour
breaking
cake flour
classifying
clear flour
gliadin
gluten
glutenin
hard wheat
high-gluten flour
pastry flour
patent flour
purifying
reducing
sifting
soft wheat
straight flour
streams
whole wheat flour

Chapter Outline

I. Introduction—This chapter emphasizes the importance of wheat flour as the key ingredient in the bakeshop. The process of milling is discussed along with different types of wheat flour. The importance of gluten and ways to control it are also discussed. Knowing which type of flour to use for specific baked goods is explored while other nonwheat flours and grains are introduced.

II. Flour Defined

III. Composition of a Wheat Kernel

IV. Types of Wheat
   A. Hard Wheat
   B. Durum Wheat
   C. Soft Wheat

V. The Milling Process

VI. Different Varieties of Wheat Flour
   A. Whole Wheat Flour
   B. Patent Flour
   C. Bread Flour
   D. Clear Flour
   E. Straight Flour
   F. High-Gluten Flour
   G. Patent Durum Flour
   H. All-Purpose Flour
   I. Pastry Flour
   J. Cake Flour
   K. Wheat Berries
   L. Wheat Bran
   M. Wheat Germ

VII. Grains and Flours Other Than Wheat
   A. Light or White Rye
   B. Medium Rye
   C. Dark Rye
   D. Whole Rye Flour

VIII. The Ancient Art of Stone Milling

IX. Getting Flour Ready for Baking: Flour Treatments
   A. Bleaching
   B. Conditioning

C. Leaveners and Salt
D. Enrichment
X. Components of Flour Important to the Baker
A. Protein
B. Starch
C. Ash
D. Vitamins
E. Moisture
XI. Defining Gluten and Its Role in Baking
XII. The Importance of Gluten
XIII. Controlling Gluten
XIV. Deciding Which Flour Is Best
XV. Storage of Flours

Review Questions and Answers

1. **Name the five stages of the milling process.**
The five stages of the milling process are breaking, purifying, reducing, sifting, and classifying.
2. **Why cannot newly milled flour be used immediately to bake bread?**
There are chemical components within freshly milled flour that produce a poor quality of gluten and a yellowish color. Over time, oxygen binds with these chemical components allowing a better quality of gluten to form and the flour turns white through a natural bleaching. Millers usually speed this process up by giving flour "chemical treatments" to ready it for baking.
3. **What is the difference between cake flour and bread flour? Can they be used to make the same type of products? Why or why not?**
The main difference between cake flour and bread flour is that cake flour is generally milled from a soft, red winter wheat and contains far less protein than bread flour, generally between 6 and 8 percent. Bread flour is a general term for flour that is milled from either hard winter or hard spring wheat and contains more protein than cake flour. The more protein a flour has, the more gluten it will form. Generally they cannot be used to make the same type of products. Cake flour tends to be used for more tender baked goods such as cakes, cookies, and pie crusts where gluten formation is not desired. Bread flour is generally used for yeast breads such as pizza and white bread where a chewy texture and gluten formation is desired. However, in small quantities, bread flour can be used successfully to increase the chewiness or structure of certain tender baked goods such as cookies, popovers, or éclair paste.
4. **Name the three parts of a kernel of wheat. Which one is used predominantly for white flour?**
The three parts of a kernel of wheat are the bran or outer hull, the endosperm, and the germ. The endosperm is the part of the wheat kernel that is used predominantly for white flour.
5. **Name the two types of protein in wheat flour that form a network of gluten.**
Gliadin and glutenin.
6. **Breads are not usually baked using rye flour as the sole flour. Why not?**
Although rye flour contains protein much like wheat flour, it does not form quality gluten and breads made with it tend to be heavy and gummy. This is because gases such as carbon dioxide cannot be held within the dough if no quality gluten strands form. Therefore it is usually combined with some form of hard wheat flour.
7. **How does the amount of protein in a wheat flour determine the texture of the baked good?**
The amount of protein in a wheat flour will determine the texture of a baked good. The higher the protein content in the flour, the more gluten develops forming a chewier, firmer texture resulting in a less tender product. The lower the protein content in the flour, the more tender and crumbly the texture of the finished product will be. This is because gluten gives strength and structure to baked goods and the higher the protein level in the flour, the more gluten forms.
8. **Why is gluten so important in the leavening of a yeast bread?**
The network of gluten is crucial to the leavening of a yeast bread. This is because the web of gluten strands throughout the dough traps gases that expand under pressure in the oven and help to leaven the bread. Without gluten, the yeast breads would be dense and flat.
9. **Which type of flour would be the best choice to make popovers? A butter cake?**
To make popovers, which are steam leavened, a flour with high-protein content such as bread flour is typically used for increased gluten development. This network of gluten helps to prevent the popovers from collapsing. A more tender baked good, such as a butter cake, will typically be made with a flour lower in protein such as cake flour or all-purpose flour.
10. **Why do white flours lack vitamins and minerals, and need to be enriched?**
White flour has lost natural vitamins and minerals due to the bran and germ layers being removed during the milling process. Millers add vitamins and minerals back into the flour to bring them back to the standard set by the U.S. Food and Drug Administration.

Test Questions

MULTIPLE CHOICE

1. Hard wheat flour can also be referred by what term?
   A. Strong flour
   B. Weak flour
   C. High-gluten flour
   D. Bread flour
2. Which part of a kernel of wheat is responsible for regenerating the plant?
   A. The bran
   B. The endosperm
   C. The wheat berry
   D. The germ
3. What part of the wheat kernel gives a brownish color to the whole wheat flour?
   A. The endosperm
   B. The bran
   C. The germ
   D. B and C
4. The first stage of the milling process where the wheat kernels are forced to be passed through two grooved steel rollers is referred to as what?
   A. The purifying stage
   B. The reducing stage
   C. The breaking stage
   D. The rolling stage
5. What determines the size of the pieces of endosperm during the breaking stage?
   A. Where the pieces of endosperm are located within the kernel will determine how soft or hard they are and how large the pieces will be when they break apart.
   B. How close together the steel rollers are determines the size of the pieces of endosperm.
   C. How dense each piece of endosperm is.
   D. None of the above
6. Of all other nonwheat flours, which one is the next most widely grown grain?
   A. Rice
   B. Corn
   C. Rye
   D. Soy
7. What is the purpose of adding conditioners to flour?
   A. Conditioners soften gluten so the fibers do not stick together.
   B. Conditioners are generally added to flour to improve the quality of gluten formation, provide the best food for yeast, and improve the qualities of the baked good.
   C. All conditioners are carcinogenic and should never be added to flour.
   D. Conditioners add vitamins and minerals back into the flour that were lost in the milling process.
8. Of all the components that make up flour, what are the five most important?
   A. The levels of starch, protein, ash, vitamins, and moisture
   B. The levels of starch, sodium, water content, diastase, and ascorbic acid
   C. The levels of minerals, protein, starch, folate, and vitamin C
   D. None of the above
9. Name three ways to control gluten development in a dough.
   A. Add fats, do not overmix, and allow the dough to rest.
   B. Decrease the fat, mix at least 5 minutes, and refrigerate the dough.
   C. Adding sugar and water while mixing decreases gluten.
   D. Adding fat is the only way to decrease gluten since it interferes with gluten fibers from joining together.
10. Why is gluten development so important in bread baking?
    A. Since gases become trapped within the network of gluten fibers, the more gluten that develops, the more gases get trapped causing better volume in the finished bread.
    B. Gluten fibers snap apart and cause breads to be nice and chewy.
    C. Gluten development causes breads to become firm and resist staling.
    D. None of the above

TRUE OR FALSE

11. _____ Patent flour contains the finest or smallest particles of flour.
12. _____ Hard patent flour contains more protein and is suitable for breads.

13. _____ Cake and pastry flour are high in protein content and are used mostly for cakes and tender baked goods.

14. _____ All-purpose flour has a higher protein content than straight flour.

15. _____ Flour is best used for baking right after it has been milled.

16. _____ Potassium bromate was a conditioner added to newly milled flour but is now banned in the United States and Europe because it is considered to be carcinogenic.

17. _____ Cake flour is bleached using chlorine gas and benzoyl peroxide.

18. _____ When a chemical leavener and salt have been added to flour, it is known as self-rising.

19. _____ Gluten is a network of proteins comprising two proteins found in rice flour.

20. _____ The higher the protein content in the flour, the more gluten it will form.

CHAPTER 4

The Science of Mixing

For video segments that correspond to this chapter, please see the About Professional Baking DVD series, Disk 1's chapter: *The Science of Mixing.*

Objectives

After reading this chapter, the student should be able to:

✓ Understand the four mixing factors that affect baked goods.
✓ Understand the three main reasons for mixing baked goods.
✓ Explain what gluten is.
✓ Explain how mixing affects gluten development.
✓ Explain how fats play a role in mixing.
✓ List the correct tools for mixing.
✓ Properly fold in ingredients.

Key Terms

dough hook
fats
folding
food processor
gluten
paddle
pastry blender
rubber spatula
whip
whisk

Chapter Outline

I. Introduction—The act of mixing or physically combining ingredients is most important to the baker. Exactly how ingredients are brought together can affect the texture of the final product. Ingredients need to be mixed in the proper order with the proper tools, following specific mixing methods to attain success in baking.

II. Four Mixing Factors That Affect Baked Goods
   - A. The Physical Act of Mixing
   - B. The Tools Used for Mixing
   - C. The Order the Ingredients Are Added
   - D. The Mixing Method Used
   - E. The Three Main Reasons for Mixing

III. Gluten Revisited

IV. Fats and Their Role in Mixing

V. The Correct Tools for Mixing
   - A. Paddle Attachment
   - B. Whip Attachment
   - C. Dough Hook
   - D. Pastry Blender
   - E. Food Processor
   - F. Whisks
   - G. Rubber Spatulas

VI. Five of the Most Common Mixing Terms
   - A. Stirring
   - B. Beating
   - C. Creaming
   - D. Kneading
   - E. Folding

VII. Properly Folding in Ingredients

Review Questions and Answers

1. **Name the four mixing factors that affect baked goods.**
The four mixing factors that affect baked goods are the physical act of mixing, the tools used, the order that the ingredients are added, and the specific mixing methods used.
2. **Name three reasons for mixing ingredients in baking.**
Three reasons for mixing ingredients in baking are to blend all ingredients into a uniform mass, to incorporate air, and to control gluten formation.
3. **How does fat in a recipe affect gluten?**
Fats are tenderizers so the more fat in a recipe, the less gluten that will develop. Fats coat gluten strands, preventing them from absorbing water and developing into a weblike structure.
4. **What is gluten?**
Gluten is a network of fibers that forms when the proteins in wheat flour (gliadin and glutenin) are mixed with water. Gluten gives strength and structure to baked goods and the act of mixing contributes to its formation. Gluten is desirable in yeast breads and undesirable in more tender baked goods such as cakes and pies.
5. **Why is it important to pay close attention to how the fat is blended into the other ingredients of a recipe?**
Fats are blended into other ingredients in different ways depending upon the mixing method used. If the fat is not incorporated properly, the texture and volume of the finished product will be affected.

6. **When would the paddle attachment be used in a recipe?**
   The paddle attachment is used primarily for creaming and blending batters for cakes, muffins, and cookies.
7. **Would a dough hook be the best tool for mixing butter and sugar?**
   No, the dough hook would not be the best tool for mixing butter and sugar. The paddle attachment would be more suitable since it is capable of combining ingredients while incorporating some air into them. Dough hooks are best used to knead yeast doughs.
8. **Which mixing tool would be best to blend the ingredients for a pie crust?**
   A pastry blender or a pastry blender attachment on an electric mixer.
9. **Why does caution need to be used when mixing ingredients in a food processor?**
   Food processors can cause ingredients to become overmixed or overheated through the friction produced.
10. **What is the proper method for folding a meringue into a cake batter?**
    First, whisk about one quarter of the meringue into the cake batter to lighten the batter. Then place the remaining meringue on top of the lightened batter. Using a rubber spatula, cut the spatula through the center of the mixtures and follow through going down to the bottom of the bowl and pulling up with the dominant hand while rotating the bowl with the other hand. This technique is repeated until the meringue is almost incorporated. The mixture should not be overmixed. A few streaks of meringue may still be visible.

Test Questions

MULTIPLE CHOICE

1. You are preparing a sponge cake batter. What is the best tool to fold the meringue into the batter?
   A. Electric mixer
   B. Rubber spatula
   C. Pastry blender
   D. Spoon

2. Which reason is not one of the three main reasons for mixing ingredients?
   A. To blend all ingredients into a uniform mass
   B. To control gluten formation
   C. To increase browning of the baked good
   D. To incorporate air

3. For what type of baked good is the development of gluten not desired?
   A. Challah bread
   B. Pizza
   C. Pie crust
   D. Sourdough bread

4. You are mixing a cake batter using the creaming method. What is the one invisible ingredient you are adding that is not listed in the recipe?
   A. Air
   B. Chemical leaveners
   C. Gluten
   D. None of the above

5. Gluten is the network of fibers that forms when what two proteins in wheat flour are mixed with water?
   A. Glucagon and glucose
   B. Glycogen and glutenin
   C. Gliagen and glutonon
   D. Gliadin and glutenin

6. You are preparing a sponge cake batter and need to make an egg foam using egg whites. What attachment should you use on the electric mixer?
   A. Dough hook
   B. Paddle
   C. Whip
   D. Whisk

7. The dough hook attachment is best used for what type of doughs?
   A. Pie crusts
   B. Yeast doughs
   C. Quick breads
   D. Cake batters

8. What is the mixing term that refers to air being incorporated into fat, often with sugar?
   A. Folding
   B. Creaming
   C. Kneading
   D. Beating

9. When folding a light meringue into a cake batter, it is important not to overmix them or the cake will not rise. Why?
   A. Overmixing is important to develop gluten and structure in the cake.
   B. Overmixing will cause a dense texture in the cake.
   C. Overmixing causes air bubbles to burst and leavening power is lost.
   D. A and C

10. How does air being incorporated into fat help chemical leaveners to leaven a baked good?
    A. The trapped air bubbles within the fat become larger because of the gases formed by chemical leaveners and help to leaven baked goods.
    B. The air in the fat does not help leaven the baked good.
    C. Fats are unable to trap air but work with other ingredients to make a smooth batter.
    D. Melted fats are best at incorporating air bubbles and working as a team with chemical leaveners to leaven baked goods.

TRUE OR FALSE

11. _____ Gluten decreases structure in baked goods, making them tender.

12. _____ The more fat in a recipe, the less gluten will develop.

13. _____ Mixing can control how much gluten develops in a batter or dough.

14. _____ Fats can aid in the leavening process by holding in air bubbles through the process of creaming.

15. _____ The whip attachment of an electric mixer is generally used to cream fat and sugar.

16. _____ The paddle attachment looks like the oar of a boat with open spaces in between.

17. _____ Beating ingredients is a more vigorous form of mixing than stirring.

18. _____ Meringues can be beaten using the paddle attachment.

19. _____ The three main reasons for mixing are blending the ingredients into a uniform mass, developing as much gluten as possible, and blending in air.

20. _____ Any flour forms gluten if enough water is added.

CHAPTER 5
Thickeners and Stabilizers

For video segments that correspond to this chapter, please see the About Professional Baking DVD series, Disk 1's chapter: *Thickeners & Stabilizers*

Objectives

After reading this chapter, the student should be able to:

- ✓ Define starch.
- ✓ Explain the role gelatin plays as a stabilizer in desserts
- ✓ Describe the three stages of gelatinization.
- ✓ List the factors that affect gelatinization.
- ✓ Describe the different types of starch and their characteristics.
- ✓ Understand how to choose which starch is best.
- ✓ Define gelatin.
- ✓ Explain the role gelatin plays as a stabilizer in desserts.
- ✓ List the three steps in preparing gelatin.
- ✓ Recognize the factors and ingredients that interfere with gelatin.
- ✓ Demonstrate how to use starches and gelatin properly by preparing the recipes at the end of this chapter.

Key Terms

agar alpha-amylase
blooming
carrageenan
gelatin
gelatinization
gelation
gum Arabic
gum tragacanth
gums
pectin
starches

Chapter Outline

I. Introduction—Starches and stabilizers are extremely important to the baker because they can be used to give desserts a specific texture, taste, and appearance. Bakers can also use starches and stabilizers to prevent any changes in texture within a dessert before it is consumed. This chapter provides a basic foundation of the principles behind gelatinization and gelation for the beginning baking student.
II. Starches Defined
III. The Three Stages of Gelatinization
IV. Several Factors That Affect Gelatinization
V. Interesting Facts about Starches
VI. Gelatin Defined
VII. How Gelatin Forms a Gel
VIII. How to Use Gelatin
IX. Other Gelatin-Like Thickeners and Stabilizers
X. Factors and Ingredients That Interfere with Gelatinization

Review Questions and Answers

1. **Name the three stages of gelatinization.**
   The three stages of gelatinization are heating the starch in a liquid, absorption of liquid by the starch, and thickening of the liquid.
2. **When certain starches are overheated or heated for too long what happens?**
   When starches are overheated or heated for too long, the molecules of starch become stretched too far, allowing the liquid they have absorbed to leak out thereby thinning out the starch-thickened mixture.
3. **What can happen if certain starches from grains like wheat and corn are undercooked?**
   When starches from grains like wheat and corn are undercooked, the mixture can have a raw, pasty taste.
4. **What is the name of the enzyme in egg yolks that prevents starches from thickening?**
   The enzyme in egg yolks that prevents starches from thickening is alpha-amylase.
5. **How is this enzyme destroyed?**
   Alpha-amylase is destroyed by cooking. This is done by bringing the starch and egg mixture to the boiling point while continuously cooking for 1 to 2 minutes.
6. **What is the most widely used starch for baking?**
   The most widely used starch for baking is cornstarch.
7. **Which types of starches thin out as they cool?**
   The starches that thin out as they cool include potato, cassava, arrowroot, and waxy maize.
8. **Name the three steps in preparing gelatin.**
   The three steps in preparing gelatin are adding the gelatin to a cold liquid, heating the gelatin to melt it down, and chilling the gelatin mixture to gelation.

9. **What are three ingredients that can interfere with the gelling of a gelatin-based dessert?**
   Three ingredients that can interfere with the gelling of a gelatin-based dessert are fresh pineapple, fresh mangoes, and fresh ginger.
10. **Why can canned pineapple be used in a gelatin-based dessert but fresh pineapple cannot?**
   Canned pineapple can be used in a gelatin-based dessert because the enzyme that prevents gelling has been destroyed through the canning process.
11. **What effect does salt have on gelatin?**
   Salt strengthens gelatin's ability to gel. This means that gelatin containing salt may set up firmer than without the salt.

Test Questions

MULTIPLE CHOICE

1. What are the two main forms of a starch?
   A. Amylase and amylopectin
   B. Amylose and pectin
   C. Amylose and amylopectin
   D. Amylase and pectin
2. What is gelatinization?
   A. The process that starches go through to thicken a liquid
   B. The process that gelatin goes through to become a jelled mass
   C. The process that gelatin goes through to thicken a liquid
   D. The process that modified starches go through when they are frozen
3. Which starch is derived from roots?
   A. Wheat
   B. Tapioca
   C. Corn
   D. Soybean
4. There are several factors that can affect gelatinization. Which of the following ingredients contains the enzyme alpha-amylase and can interfere with a starch's ability to thicken a liquid if it is not destroyed?
   A. Salt
   B. Uncooked egg yolks
   C. Cream of tartar
   D. Baking soda
5. You are preparing a pastry cream to be used as a filling for a cream pie. Which would be the best thickening agent to use, a root starch or a grain starch?
   A. A grain starch such as wheat flour or cornstarch
   B. A root starch such as potato or cassava
   C. A root starch such as soy or millet
   D. A grain starch such as rye or barley
6. How does gelatin form a gel?
   A. Once a hot liquid is added, it thickens immediately.
   B. During the melting-down stage, the network of gelatin proteins holds in moisture forming a thickened gel, which firms up as it cools.
   C. Blooming causes the gelatin to form a gel.
   D. The gelatin melts down and thickens any liquid it is put into.
7. For what types of desserts would gelatin be used?
   A. For pie crusts
   B. For stabilized whipped cream to fill cream puffs
   C. For an apple pie filling
   D. For truffles, a confection made from ganache
8. The gelling capacity for sheet gelatin is standardized. What does this mean?
   A. It means every sheet of gelatin equals 1 teaspoon of powdered gelatin.
   B. It means that one gelatin sheet equals any other in gelling strength.
   C. It means that sheet gelatin is standardly used in all restaurants.
   D. It means that for 10 sheets of gelatin, 8 fluid ounces of a gel will form as a standard.
9. When gelatin is added to a cold liquid to be rehydrated it is referred to as?
   A. A jellyfish
   B. Clumping
   C. Blooming or softening
   D. Gelation
10. What is the name of the plant gelatin that is commonly used with fondant for gum paste decorations and flowers on cakes?
    A. Carrageenan
    B. Pectin
    C. Gum arabic
    D. Gum tragacanth

TRUE OR FALSE

11. _____ Gelatin sheets are also known as leaf gelatin.
12. _____ Starches can be derived from rye, millet, barley, peanuts, and soybeans.
13. _____ When dissolving starches, they should never be heated with a liquid.
14. _____ Cornstarch is the least-used thickening agent in baking.
15. _____ Cornstarch has twice the thickening power of wheat flour.
16. _____ Salt affects gelatin by weakening its ability to gel.
17. _____ As starches thicken liquids, they absorb liquid surrounding them, burst open, and then thicken the liquid even more.

18. _____ Gelatin can originate from animals as well as plants.

19. _____ Starches can be kept indefinitely without any loss of thickening power.

20. _____ Gelatin is typically used in the making of marshmallows.

CHAPTER 6
Eggs as Thickeners

For video segments that correspond to this chapter, please see the About Professional Baking DVD series, Disk 1's chapter: *Eggs as Thickeners.*

Objectives

After reading this chapter, the student should be able to:

✓ Describe the composition of an egg.
✓ Understand the importance of proper sanitation when using eggs.
✓ Define stirred and baked custards.
✓ Explain how egg proteins become set, coagulate, and thicken custards.
✓ Describe ways to prevent curdling of custards.
✓ Demonstrate the steps to prepare a stirred custard.
✓ Demonstrate the steps to prepare a baked custard.
✓ Understand how alpha-amylase can thin custards.
✓ Understand casein and how to avoid its formation.
✓ Demonstrate how to properly use eggs as thickeners by preparing the recipes at the end of this chapter.

Key Terms

air cell
alpha-amylase
amino acids
bain marie
baked custard
carryover cooking
casein
coagulation
curdle
crème anglaise
denatured
enzymes
pasteurization
pastry cream
porous
proteins
scalding
stirred custard
tempering
thickeners

Chapter Outline

I. Introduction—Eggs are one of the most important ingredients in the bakeshop. The next two chapters explore the two main roles of eggs—as thickeners and as leaveners. This chapter introduces the egg by discussing its composition, different sizes of eggs, as well as egg products other than fresh eggs. The science behind how eggs thicken is discussed along with the preparation of custards, both stirred and baked.
II. Composition of an Egg
III. Egg Products Other Than Fresh Shell Eggs
   A. Frozen Whole Eggs
   B. Liquid Whole Egg Substitutes
   C. Frozen Egg Yolks
   D. Frozen Egg Whites
   E. Dried Eggs
IV. Storage of Egg Products
V. Proper Sanitation
VI. Eggs as Thickeners
VII. Custards Defined
VIII. Coagulation of Proteins
IX. Ways to Prevent Curdling of Custards
X. Steps to Prepare a Stirred Custard
XI. Steps to Prepare a Baked Custard
XII. Problems to Avoid with Custards

Note to Instructors: A great exercise to familiarize students with the parts of an egg is to crack an egg onto a plate (preferably black so there is a color contrast between the egg and the plate). Identify the parts of an egg, showing the chalazae and the two membranes between the shell and the egg white. An older egg and a fresher egg could be cracked and contrasts in appearance can then be observed. Observations might include the fresher egg's yolk and white stand firmer. The chalazae should appear rope-like and firm. The older egg's yolk spreads out and easily breaks apart, along with the white, while the chalazae appear thin and seem to disintegrate.

Review Questions and Answers

1. **How can you tell if an egg is fresh?**
   When a fresh egg is cracked open, the white should be firm with the yolk standing up high in the center. The chalazae should look firm and rope-like.
2. **Egg yolks contain a substance that prevents starches from thickening. What is it?**
   Alpha-amylase is the enzyme in egg yolks that prevents starches from thickening.
3. **Which part of the egg contains the fat?**
   The yolk of an egg contains the fat.
4. **Name four roles eggs can play in contributing to the final product.**
   Eggs can provide tenderness, leavening power, thickening power, and richness.
5. **What is tempering and why is it so important in the making of custards?**
   Tempering is the act of gradually adding a hot liquid to eggs without curdling them. If eggs are introduced into a hot liquid too suddenly, they will curdle forming clumps of protein in the custard.
6. **What role do enzymes play in chemical reactions?**
   Enzymes are proteins that speed up chemical reactions without being used up themselves.
7. **What happens when proteins are heated?**
   When proteins are heated, they begin to straighten out and denature. As they are exposed to higher temperatures, the strands of protein form a network with moisture held in between each strand. The proteins become firmer than before and form a gel-like substance. The proteins at this stage are said to be coagulated. If the proteins are heated even more, they squeeze out any moisture within the protein network and become clumped together and curdled.
8. **Name the two types of custards.**
   The two types of custards are stirred custards and baked custards.
9. **What is casein? Name one way it can be prevented from forming on the surface of a custard.**
   Casein is a protein found in milk and other dairy products. When casein is exposed to air, it forms a skin or crusty formation. It can appear on the surface of custards. One way casein can be prevented from forming on the surface of a custard is to place a piece of plastic wrap or wax paper directly onto the surface of a hot custard to prevent it from being exposed to air.
10. **Name three ways to prevent custards from curdling.**
    Three ways to prevent custards from curdling are not heating the custard to too high a temperature, adding other ingredients such as a starch to the eggs, and tempering the eggs to introduce them into hot liquids.

Test Questions

MULTIPLE CHOICE

1. What is the white, rope-like material that anchors an egg yolk on either side so that it remains centered within the egg?
   A. Chalazae
   B. Challis
   C. Chalazay
   D. Albumin
2. Most recipes call for what size eggs?
   A. Jumbo
   B. Extra-large
   C. Large
   D. Medium
3. Egg products must undergo a special process by law where they are exposed to a specific temperature for a specific amount of time to destroy disease-causing organisms. What is this process called?
   A. Coagulation
   B. Carryover cooking
   C. Ultra-heat pasteurization
   D. Pasteurization
4. What is the definition of a custard?
   A. Any liquid thickened by the gelatinization of starches
   B. Any liquid that is thickened by the coagulation of egg proteins
   C. Any liquid containing eggs and sugar
   D. Any liquid containing milk products, sugar, and eggs
5. As proteins are slowly heated, what happens to them?
   A. The proteins straighten out and are said to be denatured.
   B. The proteins are said to be curdled.
   C. Moisture gets squeezed out and forms clumps.
   D. B and C
6. Which of the following methods is not recommended to prevent the curdling of a custard?
   A. Tempering the eggs before adding them into a hot liquid
   B. Using a thermometer when cooking a custard to make sure the custard does not exceed 195°F (91°C)
   C. Adding water or sugar to the eggs during the preparation of the custard
   D. Using a warm-water bath to control the temperature and rate of cooking
7. A type of stirred custard thickened without a starch and used as a base for ice creams or as a dessert sauce is known as?
   A. Crème brûlée
   B. Crème anglaise
   C. Crème caramel
   D. Pastry cream
8. Egg yolks coagulate at a higher temperature than egg whites. What is the range of temperatures at which egg yolks coagulate?
   A. Between 150° and 160°F (65°–70°C)
   B. Between 140° and 150°F (60°–65°C)
   C. Between 140° and 145°F (60°–63°C)
   D. Between 180° and 185°F (82°–85°C)
9. How does the addition of water, sugar, cream, or a starch prevent custards from curdling?
   A. These ingredients when added decrease the temperature of the custard preventing curdling.
   B. No ingredient can prevent curdling.
   C. These ingredients come between the proteins and interfere with their bonds. This prevents them from getting too close and squeezing out any moisture and curdling.
   D. These ingredients absorb moisture and prevent the custard from drying out and curdling.
10. Why do many recipes for baked goods require them to be placed in a hot-water bath during baking?
    A. A hot-water bath cooks baked goods faster and more efficiently.
    B. A hot-water bath prevents the need for tempering the eggs.
    C. A hot-water bath destroys the enzyme in egg yolks, alpha-amylase.
    D. A hot-water bath helps maintain an even temperature all around the baking dish and prevents the eggs from overheating and curdling.

TRUE OR FALSE

11. ______ When preparing a baked custard, milk or cream is never scalded before adding it to the eggs.
12. ______ Stirred custards are typically cooked to 180° to 185°F (82°–85°C).
13. ______ Stirred custards are often poured through a strainer after cooking to catch any coagulated egg protein.
14. ______ When egg yolks and sugar are allowed to stand unmixed, small yellow clumps can form.

15. _____ Custards made on top of the stove are referred to as baked custards.

16. _____ All frozen egg whites are able to be beaten into a stable foam for meringues.

17. _____ The United States Department of Agriculture recommends that eggs be pasteurized to a temperature of 140°F (60°C) for 3½ minutes.

18. _____ Coagulation of egg proteins occurs at the same temperature for the yolk and the white.

19. _____ When proteins are heated for too long at too high a temperature they clump together and curdle.

20. _____ Egg whites coagulate before egg yolks at approximately 140° to 150°F (60°–65°C).

CHAPTER 7

Eggs as Leaveners and Meringues

For video segments that correspond to this chapter, please see the About Professional Baking DVD series, Disk 1's chapter: *Eggs as Leaveners*.

Objectives

After reading this chapter, the student should be able to:

✓ Define an egg foam.
✓ Identify the three types of meringues.
✓ List the tips to ensure a successful meringue.
✓ Describe and recognize the stages of egg foams as they reach soft peaks and stiff peaks.
✓ Define a soufflé.
✓ Define a marshmallow.
✓ Demonstrate the role of eggs in meringues and as leavening agents by preparing the recipes in this chapter.

Key Terms

cream of tartar
egg foams
French meringue
hygroscopic
Italian meringue
meringues
pasteurization
Salmonella
soft peaks
soufflé
stiff peaks
Swiss meringue

Chapter Outline

I. Introduction—One of the major roles that eggs play in baking is as leavening agents. Whole eggs or their component parts can hold air within their protein structure. Leavening by eggs is used in many baked goods from angel food cakes to soufflés. This chapter defines an egg foam, the three major types of meringues, and their application in baking.

II. Egg Foams Defined
III. Three Types of Meringues
 A. French Meringues
 B. Swiss Meringues
 C. Italian Meringues
IV. Helpful Hints to Get the Fluffiest Meringues
V. Using a Stainless Steel versus a Copper Bowl to Prepare Meringues
VI. Separating Eggs
VII. One Method to Separate Eggs
VIII. Substituting Pasteurized Egg Whites
IX. How to Prepare a Safe Meringue Using Fresh, Shell Eggs
X. The Trouble with Underbeaten and Overbeaten Egg Whites
XI. Defining Key Terms
XII. Incorporating Egg Foams into Other Ingredients
XIII. Defining Soufflés

Review Questions and Answers

1. **Name three ways to ensure a successful meringue.**
Three ways to ensure a successful meringue are making sure the egg whites are at room temperature; beating egg whites in a clean, dry, grease-free bowl with a clean whip; and adding a small amount of an acid such as lemon juice or cream of tartar.
2. **Of the three types of meringues discussed in this chapter, which one is the most stable and why?**
An Italian meringue is the most stable of the three types of meringues because the egg proteins are cooked as the boiling sugar syrup is added to them, helping them to set and coagulate.
3. **What does hygroscopic mean? How do the hygroscopic properties of sugar help a meringue stay moist?**
Hygroscopic refers to a substance such as sugar that can absorb moisture or water from the air. The hygroscopic properties of sugar help a meringue stay moist because the crystals of sugar absorb moisture from the air, retaining moistness, and they come between the protein strands within the egg foam of the meringue and prevent the proteins from getting too close together, which would force moisture out.
4. **Why are acids such as cream of tartar added to egg whites while beating them into a meringue?**
Acids such as cream of tartar are added to meringues to keep them stable so they do not break down and lose air.
5. **How do egg white foams work as leavening agents?**
Egg white foams work as leavening agents because the trapped air expands in the oven pushing on the batter or dough forcing it to rise.

6. **What is the temperature at which *Salmonella,* a bacteria found in some eggs, is killed?**
   Salmonella is killed at 160°F (71°C).
7. **What are the three parts of a soufflé?**
   The three parts of a soufflé are a base, which is usually a custard; flavoring ingredients; and a beaten egg foam.
8. **Why are beaten egg whites folded into other ingredients and not mixed in?**
   Beaten egg whites are folded and not mixed into other ingredients because folding is a gentler form of mixing and fewer trapped air bubbles will escape and be lost.

Test Questions

MULTIPLE CHOICE

1. Egg foams are used as a way of leavening and/or lightening which of the following baked goods?
   A. Soufflés and sponge cakes
   B. Pastry cream
   C. Marshmallows or mousses
   D. A and C
2. What is the first step in preparing a Swiss meringue?
   A. The egg whites and sugar are warmed over a bain marie and heated to 120°F (49°C) while being whisked.
   B. The egg whites and sugar are warmed over simmering water to 180°F (82°C).
   C. The egg whites and sugar are gradually cooled to 140°F (60°C) before being beaten to stiff peaks.
   D. A hot sugar syrup is prepared before it is beaten into the egg whites.
3. Of the three basic types of meringue, which one is the most stable?
   A. French meringue
   B. Italian meringue
   C. Common meringue
   D. Swiss meringue
4. Why are egg foams more stable when beaten in a copper bowl?
   A. Egg foams are more stable when beaten in an aluminum bowl.
   B. Tiny particles of copper leach out into the egg whites, which, when bound to the egg proteins, produce a highly stable meringue.
   C. A chemical reaction occurs between the alpha-amylase in the egg foam and the copper in the bowl.
   D. The copper bowl prevents moisture loss and allows the meringue to remain stable without becoming dry.
5. What is cream of tartar?
   A. Cream of tartar is potassium hydrogen tartrate, a basic salt of tartaric acid.
   B. Cream of tartar is potassium hydrogen tartrate, an acidic salt of tartaric acid.
   C. Cream of tartar is a by-product of the wine-making industry.
   D. B and C
6. Pasteurization is a process that uses what to kill bacteria?
   A. High heat
   B. Cold air
   C. A combination of high heat and cold air
   D. None of the above
7. When should a baker use pasteurized egg white product?
   A. When the supplier has run out of fresh shell eggs
   B. When the egg whites are 1 week past the sell-by date
   C. When a recipe calls for egg whites that will not be cooked to the appropriate temperature of 160°F (71°C) to kill *Salmonella*
   D. For a recipe such as sponge cake
8. What is the term that describes egg whites that are beaten to the point where the beater is held upright and egg whites stand straight up?
   A. Stiff peaks
   B. Mountain peaks
   C. Soft peaks
   D. Curled peaks
9. Soufflés are usually baked in special oven-safe containers known as:
   A. Muffin tins
   B. Ramekins
   C. Loaf pans
   D. A or C
10. The base of a soufflé is usually a custard. What does the base of a fruit soufflé typically consist of?
   A. Milk and sugar
   B. Eggs and cream
   C. Artificial fruit flavorings and meringue
   D. Fruit purée

TRUE OR FALSE

11. _____ A French meringue can be used to top Baked Alaskas or baked into a crisper meringue to be used as a cookie or as a cake layer.
12. _____ Of the three types of meringues, an Italian meringue is the least stable.
13. _____ Acids like lemon juice and cream of tartar are added to increase the volume of meringues.
14. _____ It is easiest to separate eggs while they are cold because the yolk will not break as easily.
15. _____ All pasteurized egg white products are capable of being beaten to soft or stiff peaks.
16. _____ When egg whites are overbeaten, they tend to look like soap bubbles.
17. _____ To rehydrate pasteurized dried eggs, the manufacturer's directions on the package should be followed.

18. ______ The addition of sugar to egg whites before heating can increase the temperature of coagulation.

19. ______ The addition of large quantities of water will cause a meringue to become less stable.

20. ______ Whisks are typically used to incorporate egg foams into the base of a soufflé.

CHAPTER 8

Working with Yeast in Straight Doughs

For video segments that correspond to this chapter, please see the About Professional Baking DVD series, Disk 1's chapter: *Yeast Doughs.*

Objectives

After reading this chapter, the student should be able to:

- ✓ Describe the role carbon dioxide plays in the leavening of yeast breads.
- ✓ Explain what yeast is.
- ✓ List the different types of yeast.
- ✓ Define gluten.
- ✓ Define gluten's role in baking.
- ✓ List ways to control gluten.
- ✓ Demonstrate the 12 steps of yeast dough production.
- ✓ Show how to best handle a yeast dough when shaping.
- ✓ Demonstrate how to work with yeast in straight doughs by preparing the recipes in this chapter.

Key Terms

active dry yeast
autolyse
baking
couche
degassing
fermentation
fresh or compressed yeast
friction factor
gelatinization of starches
glutathione
gluten
instant active dry yeast
kneading
lean dough
Maillard reaction
makeup and panning
mixing
modified straight dough method
osmosis
osmotolerant instant active dry yeast
oven spring
proofing
protease
punching
resting or benching
rich dough
rounding
scaling
scoring or slashing
sponge method
straight dough
straight dough method
wash
yeast

Chapter Outline

I. Introduction—Knowing how to work with yeast to prepare yeast breads is an important tool for the baker. This chapter is one of three consecutive chapters dealing with yeast breads. This chapter defines yeast, explains the different types of yeast, explains fermentation, and how yeast leavens. It deals strictly with straight doughs while the following two chapters deal with preferments and laminated doughs. Of the three chapters, this chapter is the longest because it is used to introduce many related topics while setting a foundation of knowledge for the next two. It culminates with both sweet and savory yeast bread recipes.

II. Defining Yeast
   A. Fresh or Compressed Yeast
   B. Active Dry Yeast
   C. Instant Active Dry Yeast
   D. Osmotolerant Instant Active Dry Yeast

III. Yeast and Fermentation

IV. The Correct Temperature to Ferment Yeast Doughs
   A. Friction (See Example of How to Find the Friction Factor for a Particular Mixer)

B. Temperature (See Example of How to Find the Calculated Water Temperature)

V. How Gluten Traps Carbon Dioxide Gas

VI. Developing Flavor in Yeast Breads
   A. Temperature
   B. Time
   C. Ingredients

VII. How the Amount of Water in a Yeast Dough Can Affect Hole Structure

VIII. Ingredients that Negatively Affect Yeast Breads
   A. Expired or Dead Yeast
   B. Water
   C. Salt
   D. Protease

IX. The 12 Steps of Yeast Dough Production
   A. Scaling Ingredients
   B. Mixing
      1. Straight Dough Method
      2. Sponge Method
   C. Fermentation
   D. Punching
   E. Scaling to Size
   F. Rounding
   G. Resting or Benching
   H. Makeup and Panning
   I. Proofing
   J. Baking
      1. Scoring or Slashing
      2. Washes
      3. Steam
      4. The Baking Process
      5. Maillard Reaction
      6. Completion of Baking
   K. Cooling
   L. Storing

X. Two Basic Types of Yeast Doughs
   A. Lean Doughs
   B. Rich Doughs
      1. Laminated doughs

Note to Instructors: The following demonstration provides an excellent visual representation to help students understand how carbon dioxide gas bubbles get caught within a web of gluten. First, create a "web of gluten" by knotting the two ends of a piece of string 24 inches (61 cm) long to create a circle. Interlock the string in between the fingers of both hands to create a web-like formation. Stick small Styrofoam balls in between the spaces created by the network of string. Students can then observe just how gas bubbles become trapped in a gluten network.

Review Questions and Answers

1. **Describe the fermentation process.**
   Fermentation is the process whereby yeast eat sugar and give off waste products that include carbon dioxide gas and alcohol.
2. **What is gluten?**
   Gluten is a network of protein strands that develops when the proteins in wheat flour (gliadin and glutenin) are mixed with water.
3. **How does gluten work in helping yeast breads to rise?**
   Gases produced during fermentation get trapped within the network of gluten and expand in the oven, forcing the dough to rise.
4. **Why should you be cautious when adding salt to a yeast dough?**
   Salt must be added carefully to a yeast dough because if it is added directly to the yeast, it can slow down fermentation by damaging or killing the yeast.
5. **Name three different types of yeast and how they differ.**
   Three different types of yeast include fresh compressed, active dry, and instant active dry. Of the three types of yeast just mentioned, fresh compressed yeast is the only fresh yeast. It cannot be killed by cold water and it is sold in cakes or crumbled in bags. It should be dissolved in two times its weight of warm water that is approximately 100°F (38°C) or other liquid ingredients to ensure it is evenly distributed. Fresh compressed yeast has a short shelf life.

   Active dry yeast is sold dehydrated in the form of tiny pellets or granules. It must be rehydrated in four times its weight of warm water that is approximately 110°F (43°C) to become activated. Cold water can kill or damage active dry yeast. Active dry yeast needs to be proofed to make sure it is still alive. If refrigerated, it has a shelf life of up to 1 year.

   Instant active dry yeast is dehydrated like active dry yeast, but the drying process is a gentler one so fewer yeast cells are killed. It is a more vigorous type of yeast and produces more carbon dioxide gas per yeast cell so a smaller amount can be used to get the same results in yeast breads. It does not require proofing like active dry yeast and can be mixed into dry ingredients directly without being rehydrated. If it is mixed with liquid ingredients, the temperature should be approximately 110°F (43°C) or warmer. Instant active dry yeast can be killed if added directly to cold water or a cold dough.
6. **What is the purpose of punching?**
   The purpose of punching is to deflate the dough and allow gases to escape. This step helps to redistribute the yeast to help it find fresh food and to even out the temperature of the dough so fermentation can continue.

7. **What is the best temperature to ferment a yeast dough?**
Generally, the best temperature to ferment a yeast dough is the temperature at which it was mixed (usually between 70° and 80°F (21°–27°C)).
8. **What is an autolyse?**
An autolyse is a short rest that is given to the dough after the flour and water and possible other ingredients have been mixed but before kneading has begun. The autolyse allows the flour time to absorb the liquid ingredients and form a higher quality of gluten. It also reduces kneading time and produces a bread with better flavor and color.
9. **Name the 12 steps of yeast dough production.**
The 12 steps of yeast dough production are scaling, mixing, fermentation, punching, scaling to size, rounding, resting or benching, makeup and panning, proofing, baking, cooling, and storing.
10. **How does the fermentation process contribute flavor to the finished yeast bread?**
The fermentation process contributes flavor to yeast breads because flavorful by-products are produced such as various acids and numerous other organic compounds that affect the flavor of the finished bread. Enzymatic activity controls how fast fermentation takes place. The temperature at which fermentation takes place and how long fermentation lasts also have an effect on flavor.

Test Questions

MULTIPLE CHOICE

1. Yeast is a one-celled microorganism. Where is it usually found?
   A. Yeasts exist everywhere.
   B. Yeasts are found only on fruits that grow on trees in warm climates.
   C. Yeasts are found only on vegetables like potatoes.
   D. Yeasts exist only in kitchens where baking occurs frequently.
2. Yeast requires special conditions to grow. These special conditions include:
   A. A source of food such as sugar
   B. Warmth
   C. Moisture
   D. All of the above
3. Which type of yeast is used in rich sweet doughs where there is a great deal of sugar and fat but little moisture for the yeast?
   A. Instant active dry yeast
   B. Osmotolerant instant active dry yeast
   C. Fresh compressed yeast
   D. None of the above
4. What are the two main by-products of fermentation?
   A. Alcohol and acid
   B. Alcohol and oxygen
   C. Alcohol and carbon dioxide
   D. Alcohol and enzymes that break down starches in flour
5. The temperature of three factors in the preparation of yeast doughs will determine the rate at which fermentation occurs. Which factor is the easiest to manipulate?
   A. The water temperature
   B. The flour temperature
   C. The air temperature
   D. The proof box temperature
6. When calculating the desired water temperature for a dough, the heat energy that is transferred to the dough through mixing is known as what?
   A. Heat transfer
   B. Fractionation
   C. Convection
   D. Friction
7. The fermentation process would never begin without the activity of these special proteins that break down the starches into simple sugars for the yeast to eat. What are these proteins called?
   A. Protease
   B. Enzymes
   C. Glutenin and gliadin
   D. Disaccharides
8. Which mixing method of yeast dough preparation calls for most or all of the ingredients to be mixed together at one time to make a dough?
   A. The sponge method
   B. The straight dough method
   C. The creaming method
   D. None of the above
9. A crisp, flavorful, brown crust on a yeast bread is caused by a reaction between the sugars and proteins within the dough. What is the name of this reaction?
   A. The Maillard reaction
   B. The Mailliord reaction
   C. The Malyase reaction
   D. Gelatinization
10. Why are some yeast doughs brushed with a wash before baking?
    A. Washes give breads a brown color, while keeping the dough moist so it has time to rise before developing a crust.
    B. Washes are used to keep the dough from developing a crust.
    C. Washes are used to help speed up the Maillard reaction.
    D. Washes are used to prevent too much oven spring.

TRUE OR FALSE

11. _____ Fresh or compressed yeast is killed when it is placed in cold water.
12. _____ Active dry yeast is sold as small pellets or granules.
13. _____ Yeast lies dormant at 34° to 40°F (1°–4°C).
14. _____ The ideal temperature to ferment a dough is 80° to 90°F (27°–32°C).
15. _____ Salt can strengthen gluten but can also slow down fermentation and damage yeast.
16. _____ Glutathione strengthens gluten.
17. _____ Punching the dough helps to redistribute the yeast to find a fresh supply of food.

18. ______ Benching the dough usually involves a long rest period.

19. ______ Rich sweet doughs are proofed at higher temperatures than 80° to 85°F (27°–30°C).

20. ______ A yeast dough is scored before baking to prevent the bread from splitting in the oven and giving the bread an attractive appearance.

CHAPTER 9
Preferments

For video segments that correspond to this chapter, please see the About Professional Baking DVD series, Disk 1's chapter: *Preferments.*

Objectives

After reading this chapter, the student should be able to:

- ✓ Define a preferment.
- ✓ List benefits of using a preferment.
- ✓ Understand the difference between a straight dough and a dough that uses a sponge or starter.
- ✓ Recall the differences between the various types of sponges and sourdoughs.
- ✓ Work with preferments and prepare the recipes at the end of this chapter.

Key Terms

Acetobacillus
artisan breads
biga
chef
Lactobacillus
levain
levain-levure
natural starters
poolish
preferments
retarding
sourdoughs
sourdough cultures
sponges
straight doughs

Chapter Outline

I. Introduction—In Chapter 8, students learned how to work with yeast in preparing straight yeast doughs. This chapter deals strictly with yeast doughs that are prepared using preferments. The word preferment means to "ferment before." This means that a portion of the flour, water, and yeast is allowed to ferment before the actual dough is made. Yeast doughs made using preferments are made in stages. The yeast and some of the flour and water are mixed together and then allowed to ferment for as little as 30 minutes or for as long as several days. Using a preferment gives the fermentation process a head start and contributes great flavor and/or leavening to the finished bread. This chapter will explore different types of preferments and their association with artisan breads.
   A. Straight Doughs
   B. Preferments
      1. Artisan Breads
II. Two Categories of Preferments
   A. Sponges
      1. Poolish
      2. Levain-Levure
      3. Biga
      4. Pâte Fermentée
      5. Altus Brat
   B. Sourdoughs
III. Yeast and Bacteria Living Together
IV. Reliability and Hardiness of Starters
V. Developing Flavor in Sourdough Breads
   A. Retarding the Dough

Review Questions and Answers

1. **What is meant by the term preferment?**
   The term preferment means to "ferment before." The yeast and some of the flour and water are mixed together and allowed time to ferment. This mixture is then added to the remaining ingredients to form the actual dough.
2. **Name the two reasons preferments are used.**
   Preferments are used to increase flavor and/or provide leavening for yeast breads.
3. **What are the two categories of preferments?**
   The two categories of preferments are sponges and sourdoughs.

4. **List some of the differences between a sponge and a sourdough starter?**
   A sponge is typically used up completely in the recipe and tends to use commercial yeast. A sponge can ferment anywhere from 30 minutes to several hours. A sourdough starter takes several days to make and incorporates the flavor and by-products imparted from bacteria. A sourdough starter can be started with commercial or wild yeast. After a portion of the starter is used to bake with, the remaining starter can be maintained for years without ever being completely used up.
5. **Describe how long fermentation periods and cooler temperatures benefit sourdough breads.**
   Long fermentation periods and cooler temperatures impart a great deal of flavor to yeast breads, especially sourdough breads. This is because the length of fermentation and the temperature at which it occurs controls the types of organic compounds and flavorful byproducts produced by the yeast and bacteria.
6. **Name the two strains of bacteria in a natural sourdough starter.**
   The two strains of bacteria in a sourdough starter are *Lactobacillus* and *Acetobacillus.*
7. **Why are natural sourdough starters thought to have antibacterial qualities?**
   Natural sourdough starters are thought to have antibacterial qualities because of the natural acids produced during fermentation. This acidity tends to inhibit the development of molds and other harmful bacteria, increasing the bread's shelf life.
8. **Which preferment is completely used up in a recipe—a sponge or a sourdough?**
   A sponge is short-lived and is completely used up in a recipe, whereas a sourdough starter can be maintained for years.
9. **Identify a stiff preferment that originates from Italy.**
   A biga is a preferment that originates from Italy. It is so thick that it resembles a bread dough. Bigas tend to contain more yeast to make up for their slow fermentation rate.
10. **In what type of preferment would two organisms live side-by-side?**
    A natural sourdough starter has yeast and bacteria living together side-by-side.

Test Questions

MULTIPLE CHOICE

1. Why are preferments used?
   A. To increase flavor in yeast breads
   B. To leaven yeast breads
   C. To prepare breads more quickly
   D. A and B

2. Which type of preferment is used up completely in a recipe?
   A. A sourdough starter
   B. A poolish
   C. A chef
   D. A levain

3. How is a pâte fermentée used in yeast breads?
   A. A piece of old, already fermented, dough from the previous day's batch of bread dough is added to a new batch of dough.
   B. Pâte fermentée is a fermented paste that is added to yesterday's bread dough.
   C. Old fermented bread dough is soaked in water and added to a new batch of dough.
   D. Ground up bread crumbs are soaked in water and added back into a new batch of dough.

4. The two species of bacteria that live in a sourdough starter are
   A. *Lactobacillus*
   B. Lactase and acetase
   C. *Acetobacillus*
   D. A and C

5. How is it that yeast do not eat all the available sugars in a natural sourdough starter?
   A. The natural yeasts cannot eat lactose sugar and leave it for bacteria to eat.
   B. The wild yeast cannot digest all types of sugars leaving some leftover sugars for natural bacteria to eat and thrive.
   C. Yeasts are very picky about their sugar.
   D. The yeasts are in a dormant state and cannot eat as much leaving leftover sugar for the bacteria.

6. What are the main differences between sponges and sourdoughs?
   A. Sponges take several days to prepare while sourdoughs can be prepared within a few hours.
   B. Sponges are quite thick while sourdoughs are always thin.
   C. Sponges can be kept at room temperature while sourdoughs must be refrigerated.
   D. Sponges take less time to prepare and tend to be used up completely in a recipe while sourdoughs take more time to prepare and only a portion of them is used up in a recipe.

7. Which characteristic best describes artisan breads?
   A. They use only natural ingredients with no preservatives and are crafted by hand at some stage during their preparation.
   B. They tend to be crafted by a machine.
   C. They are prepared using straight doughs only and are crafted by hand.
   D. A and B

8. In the beginning stages of preparation a sourdough starter is referred to as?
   A. A chef
   B. A levain
   C. A seed culture
   D. A and C

9. How does the thickness of a sponge affect the fermentation process?
   A. The thickness of the sponge has no affect on fermentation.
   B. The thinner the sponge, the faster the rate of fermentation.
   C. The thicker the sponge, the faster the rate of fermentation.
   D. The thicker the sponge, the more alcohol is produced with less carbon dioxide.

10. Why does a sourdough bread baked in San Francisco taste different from a sourdough bread baked in New York?
    A. Each area has its own natural yeasts that are native to that area so the yeasts native to San Francisco impart different flavors to breads baked with them compared to yeasts that are native to New York.
    B. The ocean air imparts a saltier taste to a bread baked in San Francisco.
    C. Different flours have varying amounts of enzymes in them which accounts for the difference in flavors.
    D. The amount of salt in the air varies in different parts of the country, changing the flavor of the bread.

TRUE OR FALSE

11. _____ A Poolish is typically prepared using equal parts of flour and water by weight, but the amount of yeast can vary.

12. _____ Retarding is when yeast activity speeds up.

13. _____ Yeasts lie dormant between 34° and 40°F (1°–4°C).

14. _____ Bacteria produce acetic and lactic acids during the fermentation of sourdough starters, imparting a sour taste to breads.

15. _____ Artisan breads are prepared by bakers using only machines in large-scale operations.

16. _____ Poolish is a Polish word for Polish bakers.

17. _____ A biga is an Italian preferment that is so thin it resembles a pancake batter.

18. _____ Levain-levure means "leaven of the yeast" in French and uses a poolish sponge.

19. _____ Sourdough starters need to be fed regularly to maintain a balance between the yeast and bacteria.

20. _____ Natural sourdough starters can be made using fruits with wild yeasts growing on them.

CHAPTER 10
Laminated Doughs

For video segments that correspond to this chapter, please see the About Professional Baking DVD series, Disk 2's chapter: *Laminated Doughs.*

Objectives

After reading this chapter, the student should be able to:

✓ Define a laminated dough.
✓ List three different types of laminated doughs.
✓ Demonstrate the three-fold and four-fold folding techniques.
✓ Work with laminated doughs and prepare the recipes at the end of this chapter.

Key Terms

base dough
détrempe
four-fold or bookfold
laminated dough
plasticity
three-fold or letterfold
turn

Chapter Outline

I. Introduction—This chapter deals exclusively with the three types of rich laminated or rolled-in doughs that include Danish, croissants, and puff pastry. Laminated doughs begin with a base dough. A fat is incorporated into the base dough through a series of folds and turns that create hundreds of layers. Once in the oven, the fat melts and produces a flaky pastry that can be filled before or after baking. The differences between each type of laminated dough is discussed, how to prepare them, and their applications in various recipes.

II. Laminated Doughs Defined

III. Solid Fats and Plasticity

IV. Preparing a Base Dough
   A. Danish Base Dough
   B. Croissant Base Dough
   C. Puff Pastry Base Dough

V. Enclosing Fat Inside the Dough

VI. Folding and Layering
   A. Danish and Croissant Doughs
   B. Puff Pastry Dough
   C. Why Resting the Dough Is Necessary

VII. How Laminated Doughs Puff Up and Rise

VIII. Choosing a Flour for the Base Dough

IX. Dimensions of the Base Dough

X. Tips for Successful Laminated Pastries
   A. For the Base Dough
   B. For Enclosing the Fat
   C. For Folding and Layering
   D. For Shaping, Proofing, and Baking

XI. Freezing Laminated Doughs

Note to Instructors: An easy way to visualize a laminated dough for the beginning baking student would be to take an $8\frac{1}{2}$-inch by 11-inch ($21\frac{1}{2}$ cm by 28 cm) sheet of paper and, using a pen, draw a rectangle two thirds the length of the paper to resemble the rectangle of rolled out fat as seen in Figure 10–1. Fold the paper into a letterfold or a bookfold. Then fold it again, emphasizing that with each subsequent fold, the number of layers goes up exponentially. Each student can do this to develop an appreciation of how the folding of the dough is accomplished and how the layers will look.

Review Questions and Answers

1. **Why does puff pastry dough need one more turn than Danish and croissant doughs and a different type of fold to produce its layers?**
   Puff pastry needs one more turn and a different type of fold, called the bookfold, to produce its layers because the base dough contains no yeast. So the more layers created in the dough, the more height there will be in the final pastry. The extra turn combined with the bookfold technique compensates for the absence of yeast and yields a high, multilayer, flaky pastry. Note that the bookfold creates more layers with each turn than the letterfold.
2. **Why does the fat need to be the same consistency and temperature as the base dough before it can be folded into it?**
   Ideally, the fat needs to be the same consistency and temperature as the base dough to facilitate the folding and turning process. The fat should be approximately 60°F (16°C). If the fat is too cold, it will be too hard to be evenly

distributed throughout the dough. If the fat is too warm, it can ooze out of the dough while being folded into it. If the fat is too cold or too warm, volume and texture of the final baked good will be compromised.

3. **Which two laminated doughs use yeast?**
   Danish pastry and croissants contain yeast in their base doughs.
4. **Which type of laminated dough starts with the richest base dough?**
   Danish doughs tend to have the richest base doughs because they usually contain eggs, milk, and sugar.
5. **Describe a three-fold or letterfold turn.**
   A three-fold or letterfold turn starts with the dough being rolled into a rectangle. One shorter end is then pulled one third the way up over the dough while the other shorter end is pulled over as if a letter is being folded into thirds.
6. **Describe a four-fold or bookfold turn.**
   A four-fold or bookfold turn starts with the dough being rolled into a rectangle. The two shorter sides are then folded in to meet each other in the middle. The two halves of the dough are then folded together to resemble closing a book.
7. **Name the three steps involved in preparing laminated doughs.**
   The three steps involved in preparing a laminated dough are preparing a base dough, enclosing the fat inside the dough, and making a series of folds to produce thin layers of dough with the fat in between each layer.
8. **Why should overworking a laminated dough be avoided?**
   Overworking a laminated dough should be avoided for two reasons. First, too much gluten can form, making the dough difficult to roll out and second, overworking generates heat, which can cause the fat to melt into the dough or ooze out, compromising the number of layers produced.
9. **Why should formed pastries such as Danish and croissants be proofed at no higher than 85°F (29°C)?**
   After being formed, Danish and croissant doughs should never be proofed at a temperature above 85°F (29°C) or the fat can melt and ooze out. The lack of fat inside each layer of dough will affect the volume and texture of the final pastry.
10. **Why might a high-protein flour be chosen to prepare a laminated dough when a flaky end product is desired?**
    A high-protein flour can be chosen to prepare a laminated dough to give added structure to the thin layers of dough. This produces gluten strands that have a certain amount of "give" to them so the flaky layers do not break during baking.
11. **Define plasticity and how it relates to fats in laminated doughs.**
    Plasticity is a physical property of fats and is defined as the degree to which a specific fat can be molded or shaped over a range of temperatures. The more plastic the fat is, the less likely it will melt or ooze out from the dough layers because it will remain approximately the same consistency whether the kitchen is warm or cool in temperature. This can be quite beneficial when preparing laminated doughs where turns and folds are formed repeatedly.

Test Questions

MULTIPLE CHOICE

1. Laminated doughs are used to prepare what types of baked goods?
   A. Danish pastry
   B. Croissants
   C. Puff pastry
   D. All of the above

2. Which type of laminated dough does not use yeast in the base dough?
   A. Croissants
   B. Puff pastry
   C. Danish
   D. Pain au chocolat

3. When a laminated dough has undergone all of its turns and folds, what does it resemble when cut open?
   A. A yeast dough with pockets of fat
   B. A book with thin "pages"
   C. A filled dough
   D. A and C

4. Why would overworking a laminated dough have negative consequences on the finished pastry?
   A. Overworking creates heat, which can melt the fat inside the layers, resulting in fewer flaky layers and poor volume.
   B. Overworking the dough develops gluten and results in a tough pastry.
   C. Overworking creates layers that are too thin.
   D. A and B

5. To successfully enclose the fat in a base dough, what must the dough and fat have in common?
   A. The dough and the fat should be approximately the same consistency and temperature.
   B. The dough and fat must be chilled well to ease the rolling and folding process.
   C. The dough and fat must be coated in flour to help create sheets of strong gluten.
   D. B and C

6. Why must puff pastry get an extra turn?
   A. Puff pastry is harder to work with and the extra turn gives it more structure.
   B. Puff pastry contains no yeast and relies on the extra turn and steam to leaven it. The extra turn compensates for the lack of yeast.
   C. Puff pastry contains lemon juice and water that require an extra turn to incorporate them into the dough.
   D. A and B

7. Danish and croissant doughs are generally given three three-fold turns. How else do bakers express the number of turns for this type of dough?
   A. 4 x 4
   B. 3 x 4
   C. 3 x 3
   D. 4 x 3

8. How do laminated doughs puff up and rise?
   A. The layers of fat act like spacers and melt into the dough, leaving spaces that fill with steam. The combination of yeast and steam expands the layers, separating and lifting them in the oven.
   B. The yeast in the dough rises and puffs up on the layers below, creating a separation in the dough.
   C. The rising is directly related to the low, even temperature with which laminated doughs are baked.
   D. A and C

9. Some base doughs call for a small amount of an acid like lemon juice to be added. Why?
   A. The acid gives a nice tang to the finished dough.
   B. The acid relaxes the gluten making it easier to roll out the dough.
   C. The acid increases browning.
   D. None of the above

10. Puff pastry dough should never be proofed. Why?
    A. It already has an extra turn so the proofing stage can be eliminated.
    B. Puff pastry uses the bookfold, which creates extra layers so proofing is not needed.
    C. There is no yeast in puff pastry dough so proofing is not needed.
    D. A and B

TRUE OR FALSE

11. _____ The letterfold turn is also referred to as a four-fold turn.

12. _____ Steam is the only leavening agent in puff pastry.

13. _____ Plasticity has nothing to do with how easily a fat can be molded or shaped.

14. _____ A bookfold is typically used for a Danish dough.

15. _____ It is beneficial to overwork a laminated dough.

16. _____ The sequence of rolling out the laminated dough and folding it is known as a turn.

17. _____ Resting laminated doughs in between turns relaxes gluten.

18. ______ Some bakers use bread flour to create thin layers that do not break within the dough.

19. ______ Laminated doughs are typically baked in a low temperature oven of 325°F (160°C).

20. ______ Before each turn, laminated doughs should be rotated 90 degrees so open ends are folded in toward the center.

CHAPTER 11

Working with Fats in Pies and Tarts

For video segments that correspond to this chapter, please see the About Professional Baking DVD series, Disk 2's chapter: *Working With Fats in Pies & Tarts.*

Objectives

After reading this chapter, the student should be able to:

✓ Explain the difference between the three types of pastry crusts: pâte brisée, pâte sucrée, and pâte sablée.

✓ Explain the role fat plays in making pies and tarts.

✓ List the six steps to reduce gluten formation.

✓ Demonstrate how to work with fats in pies and tarts by preparing the recipes in this chapter.

Key Terms

blind baking

docking

galette

pâte brisée

pâte sablée

pâte sucrée

stippling

Chapter Outline

I. Introduction—Fats play a major role in the preparation of pies and tarts by providing tenderness and flakiness to the crust. The three types of pastry crusts and the role that fats play in each one are discussed. Techniques used to reduce gluten formation to create the most tender crusts are also discussed.

II. The difference between Tenderness and Flakiness in a Pastry Crust

III. Choosing the Right Fat

IV. Three Different Types of Pastry Doughs
   - A. Pâte Brisée
   - B. Pâte Sucrée
   - C. Pâte Sablée

V. Six Ways to Ensure a Tender, Flaky Pastry Crust
   - A. Use a Solid, Cold Fat
   - B. Use a Low-Protein Flour
   - C. Add an Acid
   - D. Avoid Using Too Much Water
   - E. Do Not Overmix
   - F. Allow the Dough to Rest

VI. Blind Baking
   - A. Three Ways to Blind Bake a Pie Shell

VII. Helpful Tips to Roll Out a Pastry Crust

VIII. Preventing a Soggy Bottom Crust

Review Questions and Answers

1. **Describe the difference between tenderness and flakiness in a pastry crust.**
   Tenderness in a pastry crust results when the fat shortens gluten strands in the pastry crust, preventing a tough pastry from forming. Flakiness in a pastry crust results when pieces of fat evenly distributed within the dough melt in the oven, leaving spaces in which steam forms. The steam expands in the oven, forcing the dough to rise and form a flaky texture where thin layers of dough crumble apart in flakes when cut.
2. **Why does pâte sablée have to be crumbled into a tart pan and not rolled out?**
   Pâte sablée is so tender it would tend to fall apart if rolled out. It is best to crumble it into a pan and then evenly pat it down.
3. **How is the fat mixed into the dry ingredients of a flaky pie dough? A mealy pie dough?**
   For a flaky pie dough, the fat is cut into the dry ingredients until the pieces are the size of peas. The fat pieces will act like spacers in the oven creating flakiness. For a mealy pie dough, the fat is mixed into the dry ingredients more thoroughly to resemble meal and create tenderness.
4. **Name four ways to decrease gluten development in a pastry crust.**
   Four ways to decrease gluten development in a pastry crust are to use a low-protein flour, to avoid using too much water, to not overmix the dough, and to allow the dough to rest.

5. **What effect does gluten have on a flaky pie crust?**
Gluten can create a tough pastry that lacks tenderness. A certain amount of gluten is desired, however, to hold a pastry together.
6. **Describe how a pie crust forms flaky layers in the oven.**
Flaky layers are formed in a pastry crust from the small pieces of fats that are dispersed throughout the dough. The fat pieces create spaces in between the dough layers. This occurs in the oven when the fat melts into the dough leaving a space that soon fills with steam. The steam and trapped air puff up each layer of dough, separating them and creating flakiness.
7. **What can be done if too much gluten forms while rolling out a pie dough?**
If too much gluten forms while rolling out a pastry dough, the dough will become elastic and shrink back. Give it a short rest, which will relax gluten and allow it to be rolled out. Adding a small amount of an acid to the dough ingredients during preparation will help the dough to roll out more easily.
8. **What is one of the most common mistakes bakers make when preparing a pastry crust?**
One of the most common mistakes bakers make when preparing a pastry crust is adding too much water. Water mixed with wheat flour forms gluten and creates a tough crust. The less water added, the more tender the pastry.
9. **Which two types of pastry doughs require the fat to be creamed with the sugar?**
Pâte sucrée and pâte sablée are the two types of pastry doughs where the fat is creamed with the sugar.
10. **Which crust would be the flakiest—a crust made of pâte brisée or a crust made from pâte sucrée?**
The crust made from a pâte brisée dough, where small pieces of fat are dispersed in between the dough acting like spacers, would be flakier than a pâte sucrée, where the fat is blended in more thoroughly.

Test Questions

MULTIPLE CHOICE

1. Of the three types of pastry dough, which one provides the flakiest crust?
   A. Pâte sablée
   B. Pâte brisée
   C. Pâte sucrée
   D. A and C

2. How does a mealy pie crust resist moisture preventing the crust from becoming soggy?
   A. Since each particle of flour is completely coated with fat, very little water is needed to bind the ingredients together. This creates a crust that is resistant to moisture.
   B. A mealy pie dough is so tender water is more easily absorbed but cannot leak out, creating a moisture-resistant crust.
   C. The small pieces of fat act like spacers and prevent water from soaking through the flaky layers.
   D. None of the above

3. Why must the fat and water be cold when preparing a flaky pie crust?
   A. If the fat is too warm, it will melt into the dough.
   B. Cold fats have a higher degree of plasticity.
   C. If the water is too warm, it can melt the fat.
   D. A and C

4. The two types of pâte brisée include:
   A. Flaky pie dough
   B. Mealy pie dough
   C. Broken pie dough
   D. A and B

5. How does adding a small amount of an acid to a pastry dough prevent gluten from forming?
   A. The acid shortens gluten strands, making them slippery so they cannot join together.
   B. The acid denatures the proteins in the flour, preventing gluten from forming and allowing the dough to be rolled out more easily with less shrinkage.
   C. The acid strengthens gluten so much it actually weakens it, causing the dough to become more tender.
   D. The acid blocks the water from joining the proteins in the flour to create gluten.

6. Most pastry crust recipes typically call for what type of flour?
   A. A combination of pastry and bread flours
   B. Pastry flour
   C. Patent flour
   D. A combination of all-purpose flour and cornstarch

7. What does it mean to bake a pie or tart shell blind?
   A. The baker places the tart in the oven while blindfolded.
   B. A tart shell is baked with no filling in it.
   C. Dried beans are placed in the pie pan and covered with plastic.
   D. The baker has not decided what filling to put into the crust, so it is referred to as a blind shell.

8. How can puffing and shrinking of a pie crust be prevented?
   A. Dock or stipple the bottom and sides of the pastry dough
   B. Chill or freeze the raw pie shell briefly
   C. Line the raw pastry shell with parchment paper and dried beans or pie weights
   D. All the above

9. Why is an unbaked pie shell that is filled with a filling and ready to bake not filled with parchment and dried beans to prevent shrinkage before it is baked?
   A. Because the filling that is baked right in the pastry shell is enough to keep the crust from shrinking
   B. The parchment and beans would cause the filling to overflow
   C. The parchment and beans should go under the filling in the unbaked pie shell
   D. A and B

10. How can a soggy bottom crust be prevented?
    A. Use a flaky pie dough for the bottom crust to resist moisture
    B. Be sure the crust is baked long enough to prevent it from underbaking and becoming soggy
    C. Bake the crust on the highest rack in the oven to ensure even heat distribution all around the crust
    D. B and C

TRUE OR FALSE

11. _____ A more tender pastry crust forms when fat is added to shorten gluten strands, preventing them from joining together.

12. _____ The flakiest pie crust uses oil as the fat.

13. _____ A fat with a high level of plasticity creates the flakiest pastry crusts.

14. _____ Pâte sucrée and pâte sablée are typically baked blind and filled after cooling.

15. _____ Pâte sablée can be baked and eaten on its own like a shortbread cookie.

16. _____ Resting pastry doughs does not relax gluten.

17. _____ Pies can be made with a sweet or savory filling.

18. _____ The colder and harder the fat, the flakier the crust.

19. _____ When preparing pâte sucrée, the sugar is creamed with the eggs.

20. _____ Pâte sablée is referred to as "sandy dough" because of all the sugar it contains.

CHAPTER 12
Using Chemical and Steam Leaveners

For video segments that correspond to this chapter, please see the About Professional Baking DVD series, Disk 2's chapter: *Chemical and Steam Leaveners.*

Objectives

After reading this chapter, the student should be able to:

- ✓ Describe what a chemical leavener is.
- ✓ Explain the role leaveners play in baked goods.
- ✓ Differentiate between baking powder, baking soda, and ammonium carbonate.
- ✓ Describe the roles of air and steam in the leavening of baked goods.
- ✓ Define a quick bread.
- ✓ Describe the role carbon dioxide plays in the leavening of quick breads, cakes, and cookies.
- ✓ Demonstrate how to work with chemical and steam leavening agents by preparing the recipes at the end of this chapter.

Key Terms

ammonium carbonate
baking powder
baking soda
chemical leaveners
double-acting baking powder
eclair paste or choux paste
neutralization reaction
pâte à choux
popovers
quick breads
single-acting baking powder
steam

Chapter Outline

I. Introduction—This chapter introduces leavening agents other than yeast that are known as chemical leaveners. Chemical leavening agents are chemicals that react with liquid ingredients in a recipe along with the heat of the oven to produce carbon dioxide gas. The carbon dioxide gas, combined with air and steam, helps to leaven baked goods in a much shorter time than yeast. The chemical leavening agents baking soda, baking powder, and ammonium carbonate are discussed along with air and steam. Éclair paste, a steam-leavened pastry, is discussed in detail in this chapter since it is a specialty steam-leavened baked good that is in a category by itself. References to other recipes that are steam leavened within this text are also made. For example, popovers are a quick bread that appear in Chapter 13, Quick Bread Mixing Methods, but are also steam leavened. Puff pastry, a laminated dough, is also leavened by steam but appears in Chapter 10, Laminated Doughs. Specific mixing methods for quick breads and cakes are discussed in detail in Chapter 13 and Chapter 14.

II. Chemical Leaveners
    A. Acids, Bases, and Neutralization Reactions
    B. Baking Soda
        1. Shelf Life
    C. Baking Powder
        1. Shelf Life
    D. Ammonium Carbonate

III. The Important Role of Air in Leavening

IV. Steam Leavening
    A. Popovers
    B. Éclair Paste or Choux Paste

V. Two Methods to Bake Éclair Paste

Review Questions and Answers

1. **Name the three leavening agents discussed in this chapter.**
   The three leavening agents discussed in this chapter are baking soda, baking powder, and ammonium carbonate.
2. **How do baking powder and baking soda work in making a baked good rise?**
   Baking powder and baking soda both produce carbon dioxide gas through chemical reactions. The carbon dioxide gas expands in the oven, pushing against the batter or dough to leaven the baked good. Baking powder consists of baking soda and one or more acids. Double-acting baking powder, the most common type, reacts once when it comes into contact with liquid ingredients and again when it is heated in

the oven. Baking soda, a base, also known as sodium bicarbonate, requires both liquid and acidic ingredients to react to produce a neutralization reaction.

3. **Name three acidic ingredients that could react with baking soda.**
   Three acidic ingredients that could react with baking soda include: buttermilk, sour cream, and yogurt.
4. **How does steam leaven?**
   Steam is a powerful leavener that forms when the water in liquid-based ingredients comes to a boil when the temperature reaches 212°F (100°C) in the oven. When steam forms, it expands and pushes up against doughs and batters to leaven them.
5. **Why is it important to bake a quick bread right after it is mixed?**
   Is important to bake a quick bread right after it is mixed so few of the carbon dioxide bubbles (created through the reactions between chemical leavening agents and the liquid ingredients) are lost. If the carbon dioxide gas is lost, the baked good will not rise.
6. **Why is baking powder more versatile than baking soda in quick bread recipes?**
   Baking powder is more versatile than baking soda in quick bread recipes because it is double-acting and produces gas two times. Although a small percentage of carbon dioxide gas bubbles are lost during the mixing of baking powder and liquid ingredients, more gas will form in the oven. Therefore, there is not as much urgency to get the batter into the oven immediately as there is with baking soda.
7. **Why is ammonium carbonate used only for small, dry baked goods?**
   Ammonium carbonate is used mostly in small baked goods that are dry and crisp because of the ammonia it forms when it reacts with moisture and heat. The ammonia, if baked at a high-enough temperature, evaporates as the baked good cools. Larger, moister baked goods such as muffins and cakes tend to retain the ammonia, whereas the larger surface area of smaller, crisp baked goods such as cookies, crackers, or éclair paste provides a way for quick evaporation of the ammonia gases.
8. **Which chemical leaveners require heat to make them react?**
   Baking powder and ammonium carbonate require heat to react.
9. **What role does air play in helping steam and chemical leaveners to leaven baked goods?**
   Air plays a very important role in helping steam and chemical leaveners to leaven baked goods. Air is incorporated into batters or doughs through the mixing process and produces small air cells or bubbles. As the batter or dough bakes, the carbon dioxide gases and steam that form seek out those small air bubbles. The air bubbles become larger, pushing up on batters and doughs to leaven the baked good.

Test Questions

MULTIPLE CHOICE

1. When baking soda is combined with moisture and an acid, what type of reaction occurs?
   A. A fermentation reaction
   B. A neutralization reaction forming a salt, water, and carbon dioxide gas
   C. A neutralization reaction forming more acid than base
   D. A neutralization reaction resulting in an acid, a salt, and water
2. Some acidic ingredients that react with baking soda include
   A. Sour cream
   B. Cocoa powder
   C. Yogurt
   D. All of the above
3. What substances generally make baking powder?
   A. Sodium bicarbonate
   B. One or more acids
   C. Cornstarch to prevent clumping
   D. All of the above
4. Describe how double-acting baking powder reacts twice.
   A. It reacts once when acidic ingredients are present and again when it comes into contact with liquid ingredients.
   B. It reacts once when it comes into contact with liquid ingredients and again when heated in the oven.
   C. It reacts once with an acid and again in the oven.
   D. None of the above
5. Ammonium carbonate is best used in what types of baked goods?
   A. Cakes, muffins, and scones
   B. Small, crisp cookies, crackers, and cream puffs
   C. Chiffon cakes
   D. A and C
6. How does air play a central role in the leavening of baked goods?
   A. Chemical leavening agents form carbon dioxide gas, which seek out air bubbles within the batter and enlarge them. The bubbles expand in the oven creating leavening power.
   B. Air is mixed into the batter, which then rises in the oven creating leavening power.
   C. New air bubbles are created when chemical leavening agents are added to a batter creating leavening power.
   D. None of the above
7. Name some baked goods that use steam as their sole leavening agent.
   A. Éclair paste
   B. Popovers
   C. Chocolate cake
   D. A and B
8. How does a space form inside a cream puff?
   A. A knife is used to hollow it out.
   B. The egg proteins break apart from the pressure exerted on them by steam in the oven.
   C. Trapped air bubbles that form inside the dough create a space inside.
   D. B and C
9. Why must éclair paste be baked until golden brown?
   A. To prevent it from becoming soft and collapsing as the pastry cools
   B. To give it an eye-appealing color
   C. To caramelize the outside of the puff
   D. None of the above
10. Why do some recipes for éclair paste start out at a lower temperature and then, once in the oven, raise the temperature up high?
   A. The lower temperature allows the dough to rise up high before a crust forms
   B. A lower temperature allows the dough to rise more evenly
   C. To prevent the dough from browning too quickly
   D. B and C

TRUE OR FALSE

11. _____ When baking soda comes into contact with moisture and an acid, a neutralization reaction takes place.
12. _____ For baking powder to react to form carbon dioxide, an acidic ingredient must be added.
13. _____ Dutch-processed cocoa powder is acidic and will react with baking soda.
14. _____ Single-acting baking powder is used more often than double-acting baking powder.
15. _____ Cornstarch is usually added to baking powder not only to prevent clumping but also to keep active ingredients separated.
16. _____ Double-acting baking powder reacts twice in the oven to form carbon dioxide gas.

17. _____ Éclair paste must be baked until golden brown and crisp or the finished pastry could collapse and soften.

18. _____ Popovers use chemical leavening agents such as baking powder.

19. _____ Most bakers do not use ammonium carbonate for large, moist baked goods because the resulting by-product of ammonia does not have a chance to evaporate.

20. _____ When water is heated to 195°F (91°C), it becomes a gas and turns into steam.

CHAPTER 13
Quick Bread Mixing Methods

For video segments that correspond to this chapter, please see the About Professional Baking DVD series, Disk 2's chapter: *Making Quick Breads.*

Objectives

After reading this chapter, the student should be able to:

✓ Understand the differences between yeast breads and quick breads.

✓ Understand the three quick bread mixing methods.

✓ Demonstrate the quick bread mixing methods by preparing the recipes in this chapter.

Key Terms

biscuit method

creaming

creaming method

cutting

muffin method

tunneling

Chapter Outline

I. Introduction—This chapter discusses the three basic mixing methods for quick breads. They include the biscuit method, the muffin method, and the creaming method. The mixing method for popovers, a specialty quick bread, is also discussed. Differences between yeast breads and quick breads are demonstrated in a table for a quick comparison. The general goal behind quick bread preparation is to reduce gluten formation to ensure the creation of a tender baked good.

II. Differences between Yeast Breads and Quick Breads
- A. Yeast Is Alive; Chemical Leaveners Are Not
- B. Preparation of Yeast Breads Requires Time; Preparation of Quick Breads Does Not
- C. Gases are Formed before Baking in Yeast Breads; Gases Are Mostly Formed in the Oven During Baking in Quick Breads
- D. Yeast Breads Tend to be Chewy; Quick Breads Have a Finer, More Tender Crumb

III. Different Mixing Methods
- A. The Biscuit Method
- B. The Muffin Method
- C. The Creaming Method
- D. A Specialty Quick Bread—Popovers

IV. Preparation of Muffin Pans

Review Questions and Answers

1. **How do yeast breads differ from quick breads?**
Yeast breads differ from quick breads in many ways. First, yeast is a living organism whereas chemical leavening agents used in quick breads are not. Second, yeast breads require more time whereas quick breads take little time to prepare. Third, the by-products of fermentation including carbon dioxide gas tend to be formed before baking begins, whereas in quick breads carbon dioxide gases used to leaven are produced mostly in the oven. Fourth, yeast breads tend to have a chewier texture than quick breads, which typically have a finer crumb and a more tender texture.
2. **Name the three mixing methods for quick breads.**
The three mixing methods for quick breads are the biscuit method, the muffin method, and the creaming method.
3. **Which mixing method is similar to the flaky pastry mixing method for pies?**
The biscuit method of mixing for quick breads is similar to the flaky pastry mixing method for pies in that both methods require cold fat to be cut into the dry ingredients and then cold liquids are added.
4. **Which quick bread mixing method will yield a cake-like texture?**
The quick bread mixing method that yields a cake-like texture is the creaming method. The creaming method is the same method used in many cakes.
5. **How does the type of fat used in the biscuit method differ from the type used in the muffin method?**
In the biscuit method, the fat tends to be solid so it can be cut into small pieces into the dry ingredients. In the muffin method, the fat is typically in liquid form such as oil or melted butter.

6. **What causes holes and tunneling in a quick bread?**
Holes and tunneling in a quick bread are caused by over-mixing, which develops a thick gluten network. Trapped gases within the batter are unable to escape and explode inside the baked good as it is heated in the oven. The result is irregular holes and cavities that form in the finished quick bread.

7. **Why does a muffin baked without a paper liner have a nicer appearance than one baked with a liner?**
A muffin baked with a paper liner will tend to rise only as high as the liner while a muffin baked without a liner will rise up the sides of the muffin pan more easily. Muffins baked without liners tend to rise higher and look more substantial.

Test Questions

MULTIPLE CHOICE

1. What does tunneling in a quick bread refer to?
   A. The holes or cavities throughout the inside of a baked quick bread
   B. The holes or cavities of dough that form from underbaking a quick bread
   C. The tunnels that form under a muffin when blueberries or other small fruit are added to the batter
   D. Tunneling is simply the act of hollowing out the inside of a muffin with a spoon so it can be filled with jam or preserves.

2. What are the main differences between yeast breads and quick breads?
   A. Yeast breads take a shorter time to prepare than quick breads.
   B. Yeast is alive whereas chemical leavening agents are not.
   C. Gases are mostly formed before baking in yeast breads.
   D. B and C

3. Most quick bread recipes seem to give the same instructions to make sure the baker does not develop too much gluten. What are those instructions?
   A. Thoroughly blend dry ingredients together.
   B. Mix the ingredients until just combined.
   C. Fold in dry ingredients just until gluten develops.
   D. Cream the butter and sugar until light and fluffy.

4. Which method for mixing quick breads is most similar to mixing a flaky pie crust?
   A. Muffin method
   B. Creaming method
   C. One-bowl method
   D. Biscuit method

5. Which quick bread mixing method is used to develop a cake-like texture?
   A. Biscuit method
   B. Egg-foam method
   C. One-bowl method
   D. Creaming method

6. What is the technique used to combine the fat and dry ingredients in the biscuit method?
   A. Folding
   B. Blending
   C. Cutting
   D. Beating

7. In what form should the fat be when preparing flaky shortcakes?
   A. Melted and warm
   B. Frozen for several hours
   C. Solid and cold
   D. Melted, then chilled until firm

8. What causes tunneling in quick breads?
   A. Too much gluten formation
   B. When trapped gases within the batter cannot escape and explode inside
   C. When a tester is inserted too many times into the quick bread to see if it is done
   D. A and B

9. The creaming method typically uses which piece of equipment to cream the sugar and the fat?
   A. The pastry blender
   B. The paddle attachment in an electric mixer
   C. The whisk
   D. A fork and knife

10. Which of the following baked goods are referred to as quick breads?
    A. Banana bread
    B. Shortcake
    C. Muffins
    D. All of the above

TRUE OR FALSE

11. _____ In the muffin method, the fat is typically in solid form.

12. _____ One way yeast breads differ from quick breads is that chemical leavening agents are alive and yeast is a dead organism.

13. _____ The muffin method is similar to the flaky pie crust method.

14. _____ The mixing method that yields a cake-like texture in muffins and other quick breads is the creaming method.

15. _____ Most gases are formed in the oven for yeast breads.

16. _____ Quick bread batters can sit for quite a while before being baked.

17. _____ Yeast breads take more time than quick breads to prepare.

18. _____ Quick breads should be mixed for at least 5 to 7 minutes.

19. _____ Popovers are a specialty quick bread leavened only by steam.

20. _____ The "short" in shortcake refers to the short time this quick bread takes to prepare.

CHAPTER 14
Cake Mixing Methods

For video segments that correspond to this chapter, please see the About Professional Baking DVD series, Disk 2's chapter: *Making Cakes*.

Objectives

After reading this chapter, the student should be able to:

✓ Define the two categories of cakes.
✓ Describe the three cake mixing methods for cakes high in fat.
✓ Describe the three cake mixing methods for cakes low in fat.
✓ Understand the three ways to tell whether a cake is done.
✓ Prepare recipes using the various mixing methods in this chapter.

Key Terms

angel food method
cakes high in fat
cakes low in fat
chiffon method
creaming method
egg-foam cakes
emulsion
emulsifying agent
high ratio cake
immiscible liquids
one-stage method
sponge method
two-stage method

Chapter Outline

I. Introduction—In this chapter, the different cake mixing methods are discussed for cakes high in fats and cakes low in fats. Since cakes are so versatile for the baker, it is important to understand how to bake cakes properly and the different mixing methods used. Once a few basic cake formulas are mastered, the baker can create a wide range of cakes by varying the fillings and frostings. Cake formulas for each type of cake are given and additional recipes for assembling them with fillings and frostings are given at the end of the chapter.

II. Two Categories of Cakes
    A. Cakes High in Fat
    B. Cakes Low in Fat
III. Cake Batters as Emulsions
IV. Mixing Methods for Cakes High in Fat
    A. The Creaming Method
        1. How Chemical Leaveners Work with Air to Leaven Cakes
    B. The Two-Stage Method
    C. The One-Stage Method
V. Knowing Which Fat to Use in High-Fat Cakes
VI. Mixing Methods for Cakes Low in Fat
    A. The Sponge Method
    B. The Chiffon Method
    C. The Angel Food Method
VII. How to Tell When a Cake is Done
    A. Testing Cake Doneness

Review Questions and Answers

1. **Describe the two-stage method. How does it prevent gluten from forming?**
   The two-stage method is used for cakes in which a great deal of tenderness is desired. Fat is added to the dry ingredients to coat flour particles. Typically, an emulsified shortening is used because it can hold more liquid than other types of fats. Liquid ingredients are then added in two stages. The two-stage method prevents gluten from forming because when the fat is initially combined with the dry ingredients, it coats each strand of flour, which prevents much gluten from forming when water-based ingredients are added.
2. **What role does cream of tartar play in egg foam cakes?**
   Cream of tartar acts as a stabilizer for egg foams by partially denaturing the egg protein, helping to create a more stable egg foam.
3. **Compare the angel food method with the chiffon method. What are their similarities? How do they differ?**
   Although the angel food method and the chiffon method are both within the category of cakes that are low in fat and prepared with egg foams, the angel food method contains no egg yolks, fat, or chemical leavening agents and is leavened solely by air. The chiffon method contains egg yolks and a liquid fat. A chemical leavening agent such as baking powder is also added for leavening in addition to the egg foam. Both are baked in a tube pan.

4. **Why do cakes that are high in fat, such as pound cake, have a longer shelf life than cakes that are low in fat, such as sponge cake?**
   Cakes that are prepared with a great deal of fat are more tender and will retain moisture for a longer period of time than sponge cakes that contain little or no fat.
5. **What are the three ways to tell when a cake is done?**
   First, when gently pressing on the cake with a finger, it should spring back; second, the sides of the cake should pull away from the pan; and third, a cake tester inserted into the center of the cake should come out clean.
6. **Which egg foam cake typically contains a chemical leavening agent?**
   Chiffon cakes contain baking powder.
7. **What is the main leavening agent in all egg foam cakes?**
   The main leavening agent in egg-foam cakes is air.
8. **Why is the creaming step so important to the leavening of a cake? How does creaming work with chemical leavening agents to leaven a cake?**
   The creaming step is most important to the leavening of a cake because air bubbles are beaten into the fat. When carbon dioxide is produced from the chemical leaveners, it seeks out those air bubbles, enlarging them throughout the batter. These air bubbles expand in the oven and leaven the cake.
9. **What type of fat is typically used in the one-stage method?**
   The type of fat used in the one-stage method is usually a liquid fat such as oil.
10. **Describe an emulsion.**
    An emulsion is a mixture of two immiscible ingredients, usually water- and fat-based, that stays evenly blended together throughout a batter because of the addition of an emulsifying agent such as eggs.
11. **Which can hold more air—butter or shortening? Why?**
    Shortening can hold more air than butter. This is because butter contains up to 20 percent water and shortening is almost 100 percent fat and contains very little water.

Test Questions

MULTIPLE CHOICE

1. Which is not a cake mixing method for cakes high in fats?
   A. The creaming method
   B. The one-stage method
   C. The two-stage method
   D. The angel food method

2. Of the three cake mixing methods for cakes low in fat, which one uses a chemical leavening agent?
   A. The creaming method
   B. The genoise method
   C. The angel food method
   D. The chiffon method

3. Cakes low in fat are often referred to as what type of cakes?
   A. Beaten egg cakes
   B. Egg foam cakes
   C. Angel foam cakes
   D. B and C

4. Which type of fat holds the most air and is best for creaming?
   A. Canola oil
   B. Butter
   C. Hydrogenated vegetable shortening
   D. Margarine

5. Which type of egg foam cake calls for melted butter to be blended in at the end of mixing?
   A. Genoise
   B. Chiffon
   C. Angel food
   D. Butter cake

6. Chiffon cakes get their leavening from what two ingredients?
   A. Baking soda
   B. Baking powder
   C. Air
   D. B and C

7. What could occur in a cake using the creaming method if the fat and sugar are not creamed for a long enough time?
   A. The cake will have poor volume.
   B. The cake will have a light texture.
   C. The cake will become too dark.
   D. The cake will taste gritty because of the unmixed sugar crystals.

8. What is meant by a high-ratio cake?
   A. A cake with a high ratio of fat to sugar
   B. A cake that uses a high ratio of liquid to solid ingredients
   C. A cake that contains more sugar than flour by weight
   D. B and C

9. How can you tell when a cake is finished baking?
   A. A cake tester inserted into the center of the cake should come out clean.
   B. The cake sinks in when gently pressed with a finger.
   C. The cake pulls away from the sides of the pan.
   D. A and C

10. While preparing an angel food cake, what tool should be used to incorporate the dry ingredients into the egg foam?
    A. A rubber spatula
    B. The paddle attachment
    C. A large slotted spoon
    D. Any of the above tools will work if done gently

TRUE OR FALSE

11. _____ Egg foam cakes tend to be drier and more flexible than a cake high in fat.

12. _____ The two-stage method calls for emulsified shortening instead of butter.

13. _____ In the one-stage method all the dry ingredients are placed in one bowl and the wet ingredients are added in gradually.

14. _____ Oils make excellent creaming agents.

15. _____ Approximately 10 percent of shortening is air bubbles.

16. _____ Butter holds just as much air when beaten as shortening.

17. _____ Cakes made with the whole-egg foam method use just the whites of the egg.

18. _____ Carbon dioxide gas bubbles formed by chemical leaveners seek out air bubbles within cake batters making them larger.

19. _____ The ideal temperature for butter to be creamed and trap air bubbles is between 65° and 70°F (19°–21°C).

20. _____ Cakes prepared using the creaming method are quite flexible and can be rolled and filled and made into cake rolls.

CHAPTER 15
Frostings

For video segments that correspond to this chapter, please see the About Professional Baking DVD series, Disk 3's chapter: *Frostings.*

Objectives

After reading this chapter, the student should be able to:

✓ Define a frosting.
✓ State four reasons to use frostings.
✓ List the seven categories of frostings.
✓ Correctly pair cakes with an appropriate frosting.
✓ Identify the basic tools needed to properly frost a cake.
✓ Frost a cake.
✓ Prepare the frosting recipes in this chapter.

Key Terms

acetate
buttercream
chocolate confectionery frosting
egg-foam or boiled frosting
frosting
ganache
glaze
icing comb
metal cake rings or torte rings
metal false-bottom tart pan bottom
offset palette knife
palette knife
pastry bag
pastry brush
pastry tips
rolled-out frostings
royal icing
simple or flat icing
turntable

Chapter Outline

I. Introduction—Frostings or icings are sweet toppings used to fill and/or coat the top of a cake. They can transform a plain, unadorned cake from a plain dessert to an extraordinary work of art.
II. Frosting Defined
III. Four Reasons to Use Frostings
IV. The Seven Categories of Frostings
  A. Simple Icings or Flat Icings
  B. Glazes
  C. Royal Icing
  D. Buttercream Frostings
    1. Simple Buttercream
    2. French Buttercream
    3. Italian Buttercream
    4. Pastry Cream–Based Buttercream
  E. Egg-Foam or Boiled Frostings
  F. Rich Chocolate Confectionery Frostings
    1. Fudge-style
    2. Ganache-style
  G. Rolled-Out Frostings
V. Pairing the Cake with the Appropriate Frosting
VI. Basic Tools to Properly Frost a Cake
VII. How to Frost a Layer Cake

Review Questions and Answers

1. **Name the four reasons why frostings are used to cover a cake.**
   The four reasons frostings are used to cover cakes are as follows: increasing eye appeal, improving the overall flavor, enhancing the texture, and slowing staling.
2. **What determines the thickness of a ganache frosting?**
   The proportion of heavy cream to chocolate will determine the thickness of a ganache frosting. The greater the amount of heavy cream compared with chocolate, the thinner the ganache will be.
3. **Which frosting would be more appropriate to use to pipe small decorations that will harden and then be placed on a cake—a buttercream frosting or a royal icing?**
   Royal icing.
4. **Which category of frosting resembles an Italian or Swiss meringue?**
   An egg-foam or boiled frosting resembles an Italian or Swiss meringue.

5. **How do fudge-style frostings differ in preparation from ganache-style frostings?**
Fudge-style frostings differ in preparation from ganache-style frostings in that they begin with a cooked sugar mixture flavored with chocolate and butter. The mixture is cooled to lukewarm and beaten until dull. Fudge-style frostings take a greater amount of time to prepare while a ganache-style frosting is prepared simply by adding simmering heavy cream to chopped chocolate.
6. **Would a buttercream frosting be appropriate for an angel food cake? Why or why not?**
No, a buttercream frosting would be too rich for an angel food cake. In general, lighter cakes are paired with lighter frostings and heavier cakes are paired with heavier frostings. Angel food cake would be best paired with a flat icing or glaze.
7. **Which category of frostings tends to be purchased commercially?**
Rolled-out frostings such as rolled fondant and marzipan are generally purchased ready made.
8. **Which category of frostings is the simplest to prepare?**
The simplest category of frostings to prepare is the category known as simple or flat icings. Simple icings take a short time to prepare and can be used on a variety of baked goods such as light cakes, coffee cakes, cookies, or sweet yeast breads.

Test Questions

MULTIPLE CHOICE

1. Why are frostings used on cakes?
   A. To increase a cake's eye appeal
   B. To slow staling
   C. To cover up holes or cracks in a cake
   D. A and B

2. Which category of frosting is similar to a meringue, dries to a hard state, and is used for decorations on cakes and pastries?
   A. Egg-foam or boiled icing
   B. Royal icing
   C. Italian meringue
   D. Simple or flat icing

3. How is a French buttercream prepared?
   A. A boiling sugar syrup is added to beaten egg whites followed by the addition of softened butter.
   B. Egg whites and sugar are warmed and then beaten
   C. A boiling sugar syrup is added to pastry cream followed by the addition of softened butter
   D. A boiling sugar syrup is added to beaten egg yolks followed by the addition of softened butter

4. What is the fastest and easiest type of buttercream to prepare?
   A. French
   B. Italian
   C. Pastry cream based
   D. Simple

5. Which attachment of the electric mixer is used to prepare a French buttercream?
   A. Paddle
   B. Whip
   C. Both paddle and whip
   D. None of the above

6. Which of the following frostings do not require any cooking?
   A. French buttercream
   B. Flat icing
   C. Fudge frosting
   D. Italian buttercream

7. Which tool could be used to leave decorative markings on the top and sides of a newly frosted cake?
   A. A pastry brush
   B. A palette knife
   C. An acetate sheet
   D. An icing comb

8. What is poured fondant?
   A. Rolled fondant that has been heated and melted down
   B. A cooked, thick, sugar paste made from a sugar syrup that has been melted down
   C. A thin glaze made with confectioners' sugar and water
   D. A thin chocolate glaze used to dip cookies

9. How can acetate be used to coat a cake with chocolate?
   A. Acetate strips are dipped in chocolate and drawn across the cake to glaze it.
   B. A long strip of acetate, the same length as the cake perimeter, is covered in chocolate, allowed to set, placed around the cake, and allowed to harden. The acetate sheet is then peeled off.
   C. Acetate strips are used to protect a cake so the wet icing does not sink into the cake.
   D. Strips of acetate are dipped into chocolate and laid on top of the cake where they ooze over the edges, glazing the cake.

10. When is the proper time to remove a cake from the pan after baking?
    A. Hot from the oven
    B. While it is still warm but not hot
    C. When it has completely cooled
    D. After chilling it in the refrigerator

TRUE OR FALSE

11. _____ Italian buttercreams are prepared by adding a boiling sugar syrup to beaten egg whites followed by the addition of softened butter.

12. _____ Simple icings are cooked very quickly.

13. _____ Glazes are thick and need to be spread on cakes using a palette knife.

14. _____ Ganache-style frostings take longer to prepare than a fudge frosting.

15. _____ Royal icing tends to be used to prepare decorations for cakes rather than as an icing to frost a cake.

16. _____ Marzipan and modeling chocolate are known as rolled-out frostings.

17. _____ Metal cake rings or torte rings can be used to hold cake layers filled with soft fillings until they become firm.

18. _____ It is best to frost a cake while it is warm.

19. _____ A simple buttercream requires some cooking.

20. _____ A dense chocolate cake is best paired with a richer frosting.

CHAPTER 16
Cookies

For video segments that correspond to this chapter, please see the About Professional Baking DVD series, Disk 3's chapter: *Cookies.*

Objectives

After reading this chapter, the student should be able to:

✓ Define a cookie.
✓ List the eight categories of cookies.
✓ Explain the three basic cookie mixing methods.
✓ Manipulate ingredients to attain desirable cookie characteristics.
✓ Prepare the recipes at the end of this chapter.

Key Terms

bar cookies
cookies
creaming method
drop cookies
egg-foam method
molded cookies
one-bowl method
piped cookies
refrigerator cookies
rolled cookies
sheet cookies
wafer cookies

Chapter Outline

I. Introduction—Cookies are defined as a diverse group of small, sweet cakes or pastries that are described and categorized by how the dough is prepared and shaped for baking. Although cookies share many of the same mixing methods as cakes, the diversity of recipes for cookies is without limits. By characteristics, cookies range anywhere from soft and chewy to crisp and crunchy. This chapter emphasizes specific desired characteristics in cookies and how to achieve them through the manipulation of ingredients.

II. Categories of Cookies
   A. Drop Cookies
   B. Refrigerator Cookies
   C. Molded Cookies
   D. Bar Cookies
   E. Sheet Cookies
   F. Rolled Cookies
   G. Piped Cookies
   H. Wafer Cookies

III. Three Basic Cookie Mixing Methods
   A. Creaming Method
   B. One-Bowl Method
   C. Egg-Foam Method

IV. Understanding the Characteristics of Cookies and How to Manipulate Them
   A. Crisp
   B. Soft
   C. Chewy
   D. Brown
   E. Pale
   F. Spread
   G. Increased Spread
   H. Decreased Spread

V. Tips for Making Successful Cookies

Review Questions and Answers

1. **What are hygroscopic sugars?**
   Hygroscopic sugars are sugars that absorb moisture from the surrounding air. They include brown sugar, molasses, corn syrup, and honey.
2. **Why do cookies containing brown sugar, molasses, corn syrup, or honey become soft after baking?**
   Cookies that contain hygroscopic sugars such as brown sugar, molasses, corn syrup, or honey absorb moisture from the air and because of this additional moisture remain soft after baking.
3. **How does the protein content of a flour affect a cookie's texture?**
   The protein content of a flour can affect a cookie's texture. Generally, flours that contain high amounts of protein are able to absorb more water from the wet ingredients and produce a drier, crisper cookie. Flours that contain lower amounts of protein cannot absorb as much water. The unabsorbed water forms steam in the oven and causes the cookies to become soft and puffy.

4. **What is the mixing method used when making lady fingers or meringue cookies?**
   The mixing method used for lady fingers or meringue cookies is the egg-foam method.
5. **Name the eight categories of cookies.**
   The eight categories of cookies are drop cookies, refrigerator cookies, molded cookies, bar cookies, sheet cookies, rolled cookies, piped cookies, and wafer cookies.
6. **Why is baking soda used to help make cookies browner and crisper?**
   Baking soda is used to help make cookies browner and crisper. Since acidic doughs do not brown well and baking soda neutralizes acidity, cookies that contain baking soda will brown faster. Baking soda also weakens gluten within the dough. This causes cookies to spread out more during baking and cookies with more spread tend to be crisper.
7. **Name the three basic mixing methods used in cookie preparation.**
   The three basic mixing methods used for cookie preparation are the creaming method, the one-bowl method, and the egg-foam method.
8. **Why does cake flour produce a paler cookie?**
   Cake flour produces a paler cookie because it is bleached and acidic. Since acidic batters do not brown well, a paler cookie is the result.
9. **How are wafer cookies or tuiles able to be formed into different shapes without breaking?**
   Wafer cookies or tuiles are able to be formed into different shapes without breaking because they are quite flexible while still hot from the oven. Once they cool, the sugar within the cookie recrystallizes and hardens producing their characteristic crispness.

Test Questions

MULTIPLE CHOICE

1. Which definition defines "cookies" the best?
   A. Cookies are defined as small cakes frosted with icing.
   B. Cookies are defined as small cakes, less than 4 inches (10 cm) in diameter that may or may not be frosted.
   C. Cookies are defined as small, sweet cakes placed into categories by how the dough is prepared and shaped for baking.
   D. Cookies are defined as small cakes such as brownies, lady fingers, and chocolate chip.

2. Which category of cookie is one of the most labor-intensive?
   A. Drop
   B. Wafer
   C. Rolled
   D. Molded

3. Name a type of bar cookie that can be quite hard and is typically dipped into coffee or wine to soften it.
   A. Tuiles
   B. Brown sugar pecan refrigerator cookies
   C. Espresso almond biscotti
   D. None of the above

4. What is another term that can be used to describe a wafer cookie batter?
   A. Tulipe batter
   B. Thin brownie batter
   C. Stencil batter
   D. A and C

5. What causes wafer cookies to harden to a crisp and crunchy texture as they cool?
   A. The melted sugar in the batter recrystallizes and hardens
   B. The high fat content causes the cookies to harden
   C. Egg whites added to the batter contribute to a crisp cookie
   D. All of the above

6. Which of the mixing methods below is used for cookies?
   A. The two-stage method
   B. The egg-foam method
   C. The one-bowl method
   D. B and C

7. You are preparing drop cookies using the creaming method of mixing. What type of fat would be best to use if you desire a crisper texture?
   A. Butter
   B. Vegetable shortening
   C. Lard
   D. Emulsified shortening

8. You wish to prepare a cookie with little color. What are some ingredients that may help you achieve this goal?
   A. Using a high-protein flour such as bread flour
   B. Using a low-protein flour such as cake flour
   C. Using baking soda
   D. Using brown sugar

9. Given the fact that acidic cookie doughs do not brown as well as less acidic doughs, what ingredients can be added to a cookie recipe to increase browning?
   A. Add a flour with a low-protein content
   B. Add baking powder
   C. Add baking soda
   D. Add honey, which contains fructose, a fruit sugar

10. What happens to a cookie that contains a large amount of baking soda?
    A. The cookie will brown more easily.
    B. The cookie will spread, producing a crisper cookie.
    C. A and B
    D. The cookie will be pale and chewy.

TRUE OR FALSE

11. _____ Cookies are always easily categorized by type and mixing method used.

12. _____ Not all cookies use chemical leaveners.

13. _____ Refrigerator cookies are typically rolled into logs before being chilled and sliced for baking.

14. _____ Wafer cookies are soft and chewy when baked.

15. _____ All wafer cookies spread out in the oven.

16. _____ Using a fat with a high melting point contributes to a crisper cookie.

17. _____ Hygroscopic sugars are used to prepare cookies with a crisp texture.

18. _____ Freshly baked cookies may appear soft and underbaked while hot from the oven and firm up as they cool.

19. _____ A greased sheet pan causes cookies to spread.

20. _____ Solid vegetable shortening is used in cookies where less spread is desired.

CHAPTER 17
Building Blocks with Sugar

For video segments that correspond to this chapter, please see the About Professional Baking DVD series, Disk 3's chapter: *Building Blocks With Sugar.*

Objectives

After reading this chapter, the student should be able to:

- ✓ Demonstrate the three basic steps to prepare sugar syrups for desserts and confections.
- ✓ Recognize when a sugar syrup is done.
- ✓ Describe the process of crystallization.
- ✓ List three ways to control crystallization.
- ✓ Prepare caramelized sugar using the dry method and the wet method.
- ✓ Prepare the recipes in this chapter.

Key Terms

caramelized sugar
cold-water test
crystallization
dry method
interfering agents
inversion
simple syrup
solute
solution
solvent
sucrose
sugar syrup
wet method

Chapter Outline

I. Introduction—Sugar, a crystalline substance is one of the most widely used ingredients in baking. By melting sugar, cooking it, and changing its chemical structure the baker can learn to control the crystallization process. This chapter explores the process of crystallization and how to prepare sugar syrups as the foundation of a vast array of desserts and confections.

II. Three Basic Steps in Preparing Sugar Syrups for Desserts and Confections
    A. Dissolving Sugar in Water
        1. Simple Syrups
    B. Concentrating the Sugar Syrup
    C. Cooling the Sugar Syrup

III. Two Ways to Determine When a Sugar Syrup is Done

IV. Understanding the Process of Crystallization

V. Ways to Control Crystallization
    A. Adding an Interfering Agent
        1. Interfering Agents Added During the Preparation of Sugar Syrups
        2. Interfering Agents Added After Cooking Sugar Syrups
    B. Keeping Stirring to a Minimum
    C. Preventing Crystals from Forming on the Sides of the Pot

VI. Two Methods to Prepare Caramel
    A. The Wet Method
    B. The Dry Method

VII. Where Caramel Gets Its Flavor

VIII. Using Caution When Working with Sugar

IX. Tips for Preparing Sugar Syrups

X. Storage of Confections Made from Caramel

Review Questions and Answers

1. **Name the three basic steps to prepare a sugar syrup.**
   The three basic steps to prepare a sugar syrup include dissolving the sugar in water, concentrating the sugar syrup by cooking it, and cooling the sugar syrup.
2. **Name the two parts of a solution.**
   The two parts of a solution include the solute, the substance that is being dissolved which is usually a solid, and the solvent, the liquid that the substance is placed into to help it to dissolve.
3. **How can a baker dissolve a large amount of sugar in water?**
   A baker can dissolve a large amount of sugar in water by heating the water. The warmer the water, the more sugar that can be dissolved into it because the faster the molecules of sugar move in the solution, the less likely they will form crystals by joining together and settling out of solution.

4. **Which is more desirable in a candy, small or large sugar crystals? Why?**
   Small sugar crystals are desirable in a candy because they are less detectable on the tongue. Candies and confections with small sugar crystals taste smooth and creamy.
5. **Why should a bowl of ice water be kept next to the stovetop when preparing a sugar syrup?**
   A bowl of ice water should always be kept next to the stovetop when preparing a sugar syrup because sugar syrups are quite sticky and they can stick to the skin easily. Also, the high temperatures reached by sugar syrups can cause severe burns. Therefore it is wise to have a bowl of ice water nearby to immediately cool the sugar syrup down if it accidentally splatters onto a finger or a hand.
6. **What is an interfering agent?**
   An interfering agent is an ingredient that prevents sugar crystals from forming during the preparation of sugar syrups. They can be added during the preparation of a sugar syrup and include such ingredients as corn syrup or an acid. Interfering agents can also be added after the sugar syrup is finished cooking. Such interfering agents include high-fat ingredients such as heavy cream, butter, eggs, or chocolate.
7. **Describe the process of inversion and how it can help bakers and confectioners control crystallization.**
   Inversion is the process of heating sugar (sucrose) with an acid. As sucrose is heated in the presence of an acid, it breaks down into its two component sugars, glucose and fructose. Since having two sugars present creates an impure state, crystallization will not occur as readily. Inversion helps to keep candies and confections smooth by keeping crystals small and to a minimum.
8. **What are the advantages to preparing caramelized sugar using the wet method versus the dry method?**
   The biggest advantage to preparing caramelized sugar using the wet method is that the risk of burning the sugar is greatly reduced since the sugar is dissolved in water during the cooking process.
9. **Why is heavy cream and not skim milk added to caramelized sugar to prevent crystals from forming?**
   Heavy cream is added to caramelized sugar instead of skim milk because the high fat content is necessary to coat the sugar molecules to prevent them from joining together to form large crystals. The high temperatures reached by many sugar syrups would cause the proteins in skim milk to curdle.

Test Questions

MULTIPLE CHOICE

1. Which of the steps below is not one of the basic steps needed to prepare a sugar syrup?
   A. Concentrating the sugar syrup
   B. Heating the sugar syrup to the soft-ball stage 235° to 240°F (113°–115°C)
   C. Cooling the sugar syrup
   D. Dissolving sugar in water

2. What is the cold-water test?
   A. A test to determine the correct temperature of a sugar syrup that consists of placing a drop of syrup into a glass of cold water and then gathering it into a ball
   B. A test where a drop of cold water is added to the sugar syrup to see how hot it becomes
   C. When a thermometer is placed into cold water first before placing it into a sugar syrup
   D. None of the above

3. If a sugar syrup is simply sugar dissolved in water, which of these ingredients is known as the solute?
   A. The water
   B. The sugar
   C. A and B
   D. None of the above

4. What is a simple syrup used for?
   A. To moisten cake layers
   B. As part of the base for a frozen dessert such as a sorbet
   C. To glaze the tops of pastries such as Danish
   D. All of the above

5. What happens to a sugar syrup as it boils?
   A. Water evaporates.
   B. The sugar syrup becomes more and more concentrated.
   C. All of the sugar dissolves.
   D. All of the above

6. Why is very dark caramelized sugar unable to firm up again and recrystallize?
   A. Because only small sugar crystals form at high temperatures and cannot join together to firm up
   B. Because chemical changes between the saucepan and the sugars form unstable compounds
   C. Because so many chemical changes have occurred in the sugar that there is no original sugar left to recrystallize and firm up
   D. None of the above

7. Which of the following will help to prevent crystals from forming when preparing a sugar syrup?
   A. Corn syrup
   B. Lemon juice
   C. Skim milk
   D. A and B

8. The process of inversion creates an impure state resulting in little or no crystallization. Which one of the following describes the process of inversion?
   A. A base heated with sugar
   B. Fructose heated with sugar
   C. An acid heated with sugar
   D. Levulose heated with sugar

9. Name the two methods to prepare caramel.
   A. The moist method
   B. The dry method
   C. The wet method
   D. B and C

10. What contributes to the great flavor of caramel?
    A. Keeping crystallization to a minimum
    B. The fermentation reaction
    C. The Maillard reaction
    D. The evaporation of water into the air during the boiling of sugar syrups

TRUE OR FALSE

11. _____ Stirring a sugar syrup encourages crystals to form.

12. _____ Too much corn syrup can prevent any crystallization from occurring, which can prevent certain candies from hardening to the proper consistency.

13. _____ The faster a sugar syrup cools, the smaller the sugar crystals that form.

14. _____ Inversion is the process where baking soda is heated with sucrose to prevent crystallization.

15. _____ Caramel decorations can be stored at room temperature with a desiccant.

16. _____ Minerals in tap water can cause sugar syrups to brown faster.

17. _____ Large sugar crystals are more desirable in a caramel sauce.

18. _____ The deeper the color in a boiling sugar syrup, the greater the chemical changes that are occurring to the sugars.

19. _____ Once caramelized sugar reaches the correct temperature, it can sit for up to one hour before being used or combined with other ingredients.

20. _____ When a sugar syrup cools, the size of the crystals that form will determine the color and texture of the final product.

CHAPTER 18
Frozen Desserts

For video segments that correspond to this chapter, please see the About Professional Baking DVD series, Disk 3's chapter: *Dessert Sauces & Plating.*

Objectives

After reading this chapter, the student should be able to:

✓ Explain the difference between churn-frozen and still-frozen desserts.

✓ Explain the factors that contribute to texture in frozen desserts.

✓ Describe the roles that sugar and salt play in preparing frozen desserts.

✓ Demonstrate how to prepare the churn-frozen and still-frozen desserts in this chapter.

Key Terms

bombe
churn-frozen
granité (granita)
mousse
mouthfeel
overrun
parfait
semifreddo
sherbet
sorbet
still-frozen

Chapter Outline

I. Introduction—There are a wide variety of frozen desserts that range anywhere from a simple sorbet or granité to a rich and creamy ice cream or semifreddo. This chapter explores the different categories of frozen desserts, their preparation, and the different factors that affect their texture and taste.

II. The Importance of Good Sanitation When Preparing Frozen Desserts

III. Two Categories of Frozen Desserts

IV. Churn-Frozen Desserts
- A. Ice Cream
- B. Gelato
- C. Frozen Yogurt
- D. Sorbet
- E. Sherbet

V. Why Churning Is So Important

VI. Between Churn-Frozen and Still-Frozen

VII. Still-Frozen Desserts

VIII. Factors that Contribute to Texture
- A. Size of Ice Crystals
- B. Amount of Fat
- C. Incorporation of Air
- D. Emulsifiers and Stabilizers
- E. Aging

IX. Summing up Texture with Mouthfeel

X. Building Flavors in Frozen Desserts

XI. The Power of Sugar and Salt in Preparing Frozen Desserts
- A. Sugar
- B. Salt

XII. Tips for Preparing Successful Frozen Desserts

Review Questions and Answers

1. **What is the difference between a churn-frozen dessert and a still-frozen dessert?**
Churn-frozen desserts are constantly stirred or rotated as they freeze while still-frozen desserts freeze without any stirring or churning.

2. **What role does sugar play in the preparation of a frozen dessert such as a sorbet versus a granité?**
Sugar plays a major role in frozen desserts such as sorbets and granités because the specific amount of sugar will determine how hard the final product will be. The more sugar that a frozen dessert base contains, the less solid it will freeze. This is because sugar depresses the freezing point of water making it freeze at a lower temperature than it would normally. Sorbets typically contain twice the amount of sugar than a granité would have because a sorbet's consistency is generally soft and scoopable. A granité typically has an icier, coarser consistency so not as much sugar is needed.

3. **Name the five factors that contribute to the texture of a frozen dessert.**
The five factors that contribute to the texture of a frozen dessert are the size of the ice crystals formed, the amount of fat in the base, the incorporation of air into the base as it freezes, any emulsifiers or stabilizers that are added, and the aging of the base.

4. **What is *mouthfeel?***
   Mouthfeel is the term used to describe how a food tastes and feels in the mouth and on the tongue. Frozen desserts should melt in the mouth into a smooth, creamy liquid that is pleasant, with little graininess.
5. **What is *overrun* and why is it so important to the texture of a churn-frozen dessert?**
   Overrun is the increase in volume of an ice cream base that occurs during the freezing process through the incorporation of air from churning. Overrun is expressed as a percentage. A certain percentage of overrun is necessary to create a light, airy texture. However, too much overrun can create a foamy texture, which is undesirable, whereas too little overrun creates a dense, coarse texture.
6. **Name the three types of bases from which a still-frozen dessert can be made.**
   The three types of bases from which a still-frozen dessert can be made are a custard base, an Italian meringue base, and a fruit base.
7. **Why do frozen desserts need to be flavored more boldly than other desserts served warm or at room temperature?**
   Frozen desserts need to be more boldly flavored than warm or room temperature desserts because their frozen temperatures dull flavors. The molecules that make up frozen desserts move more slowly than the molecules that make up warmer foods. This means that those colder molecules reach nerve endings in the nose and taste buds at a slower rate.
8. **How does chilling the base before freezing create a smoother texture in the finished product?**
   Chilling the base before freezing creates a smoother texture in the finished product because the base will freeze faster and with smaller ice crystals, producing a silkier texture.
9. **Why is good sanitation so important in the preparation of frozen desserts?**
   Sanitation is very important in the preparation of frozen desserts because many frozen dessert bases are prepared from custards. Custards containing eggs and dairy products are especially susceptible to bacterial growth. All ingredients should be kept at proper temperatures and all equipment and utensils should be washed and sanitized thoroughly before and after use.
10. **How does a semifreddo differ from a sorbet?**
    A semifreddo is a still-frozen dessert that begins with a custard base to which whipped cream or beaten egg whites are added to increase volume and lighten the texture of the finished product. The mixture is then poured into a container or small molds. It is then frozen until firm. A sorbet, on the other hand, is a churn-frozen dessert that contains no dairy products. A sorbet is typically made from fruit purées sweetened with a sugar syrup and, unlike a semifreddo, they tend to be firmer in texture and lower in fat.
11. **What is *aging* and how does it improve the flavor of frozen desserts?**
    When a frozen dessert base is refrigerated for several hours before it has undergone the freezing process, it is referred to as aging. Aging improves the flavor and texture of a frozen dessert by not only allowing the flavors to intermingle but it allows proteins within the base to bind with water creating a smoother, creamier texture once it has gone through the freezing process.

Test Questions and Answers

MULTIPLE CHOICE

1. Most ice creams start out with a base that contains what ingredients?
   A. Eggs, milk and/or cream, sugar, and flavorings
   B. Fruit purée, sugar, sugar syrup
   C. Egg whites beaten into a meringue and filled into whipped cream
   D. Eggs, yogurt, sugar, and flavorings
2. What is the minimum percentage of milk fat an ice cream must contain by law?
   A. 20 percent
   B. 10 percent
   C. 50 percent
   D. 100 percent
3. What is overrun?
   A. When the volume of frozen base runs over the edges of the container it is in
   B. When fat from the cream in the base rises to the top
   C. When the freezer the base is being stored in is too full
   D. When air is incorporated into the base through the churning process
4. Whether or not a frozen dessert develops a smooth and creamy texture is dependent on which of the following factors?
   A. The size of ice crystals that form during freezing
   B. The number of egg yolks added to the base
   C. The incorporation of air into the base as it freezes
   D. A and C
5. Which group of ingredients best describes what a strawberry semifreddo prepared from a fruit base may contain?
   A. Frozen strawberries, sugar syrup, and heavy cream
   B. Puréed strawberries, cooked custard, strawberry preserves
   C. Sugar syrup, puréed strawberries, yogurt
   D. Milk, egg whites, and strawberry extract
6. Why is sugar so critical to the preparation of frozen desserts?
   A. Sugar elevates the freezing point of water causing it to freeze at a higher temperature.
   B. The small crystalline structure of sugar makes it ideal to dissolve in all types of frozen dessert bases.
   C. Sugar depresses the freezing point of water and prevents a frozen dessert from freezing too hard.
   D. Sugar makes the dessert taste good.
7. Frozen desserts are best stored at what temperature range?
   A. Between –10° and 0°F (–24° and –18°C)
   B. Between 10° and 32°F (–12° and 0°C)
   C. Between 0° and 10°F (–18° and –12°C)
   D. Between –10° and 10°F (–24° and –12°C)
8. How are sorbets often served?
   A. As a palate cleanser or intermezzo
   B. As a filling for a tart shell
   C. As a light dessert in the summertime
   D. A and C
9. How are granités or granitas prepared for service?
   A. They are scooped into sundae glasses with an ice cream scooper.
   B. They are scraped with a fork to create icy shards and served in a dessert glass.
   C. They are scooped into dessert glasses and filled with champagne.
   D. They are scraped with a serrated knife and served topped with whipped cream.
10. What is the purpose of aging a frozen dessert base?
    A. Aging promotes good bacterial growth, which contributes to flavor.
    B. Aging creates a smoother texture because the proteins within the base bind with water.
    C. Aging causes egg proteins to coagulate and thicken.
    D. Aging should not be done because it contributes to an icy texture.

TRUE OR FALSE

11. _____ Emulsifiers and stabilizers may be added to commercial ice cream bases to prevent the separation of ingredients.
12. _____ Sherbets contain only fruit purées and no milk.
13. _____ Smaller ice crystals taste best on the tongue because they are barely noticeable.
14. _____ Sorbets are known as still-frozen desserts.
15. _____ Churn-frozen desserts should be frozen slowly.
16. _____ The can of an ice cream machine should never be filled more than two-thirds full.
17. _____ Granités are smooth and creamy in texture.
18. _____ Aging the base can improve the texture.

19. _____ A semifreddo is a custard base with beaten egg whites and/or whipped cream folded in.

20. _____ Ice creams with a 100 percent overrun are always of the highest quality.

CHAPTER 19
Chocolate

For video segments that correspond to this chapter, please see the About Professional Baking DVD series, Disk 3's chapter: *Chocolate.*

Objectives

After reading this chapter, the student should be able to:

- ✓ Understand the process of chocolate making.
- ✓ Know the differences between milk, semisweet, and white chocolates.
- ✓ Define how cocoa butter affects the quality of chocolate.
- ✓ Demonstrate what tempering is.
- ✓ List the difficulties of working with chocolate.
- ✓ Demonstrate how to prepare the recipes in this chapter.

Key Terms

baking chocolate
bittersweet chocolate
bloom
cacao beans
chocolate
chocolate liquor
cocoa butter
compound coating
couverture
Dutch processed cocoa powder
ganache
milk chocolate
natural cocoa powder
nibs
seizing
semisweet chocolate
tempering
unsweetened chocolate
white chocolate

Chapter Outline

I. Introduction—Chocolate and chocolate desserts are some of the most popular items that a restaurant menu can offer. It is important for bakers and pastry chefs to understand the origins of chocolate and how to use it successfully in recipes and how to create a variety of decorations and confections.

II. The Origins of Chocolate

III. Cocoa Butter and Mouthfeel

IV. The Most Common Types of Chocolate
- A. Unsweetened Chocolate
- B. Milk Chocolate
- C. Semisweet and Bittersweet Chocolate
- D. Couverture
- E. Cocoa Powder
- F. White Chocolate
- G. Chocolate Chips
- H. Imitation Chocolate-Flavored Products
- I. Imitation White Chocolate–Flavored Products

V. Water and Chocolate

VI. Properly Melting Chocolate

VII. The Fat Crystals in Cocoa Butter

VIII. Why Chocolate Is Tempered

IX. Determining When Tempering Is Necessary

X. Tempering

XI. Two Methods of Tempering
- A. Method 1: The Table Method
- B. Method 2: The Seeding or Injection Method

XII. Determining When the Chocolate is Tempered

XIII. Commercial Tempering Machines

XIV. What to Do with Tempered Chocolate

XV. Blooming
- A. Sugar Bloom
- B. Fat Bloom

XVI. Ganache

XVII. Dense versus Light Truffle Centers
- A. Dense Truffles
- B. Light Truffles

XVIII. Molding Chocolate
- A. Chocolate Molds

Review Questions and Answers

1. **What causes the whitish-gray covering to form on some chocolate?**
When tempered chocolate is exposed to changes in temperature and humidity, a whitish-gray covering can form. This is known as bloom. There are two types of bloom. The first type, sugar bloom, can occur when the sugar crystals within the chocolate are exposed to moisture, which causes them to rise to the surface and recrystallize. The second type of

bloom known as fat bloom occurs when crystals of fat migrate to the surface and recrystallize on the outside.

2. **Where does cocoa powder come from?**
Cocoa powder is produced when cocoa butter is pressed out of chocolate liquor forming a dry, powdery residue.
3. **Which type of cocoa powder reacts with baking soda to produce carbon dioxide gas, which can be used to leaven baked goods?**
The natural-forming cocoa powder is acidic and reacts with baking soda to leaven baked goods.
4. **Why is the addition of cocoa butter so important to the quality of chocolate?**
Cocoa butter, the natural fat found in chocolate, is an important factor in determining the quality of chocolate. The higher the quantity of cocoa butter in chocolate, the silkier and smoother the chocolate and the higher its quality. This is mainly due to cocoa butter's melting point, which is slightly below human body temperature.
5. **What is white chocolate?**
White chocolate is actually not chocolate in the true sense of the word since it contains no chocolate liquor. It is actually a candy composed of cocoa butter and/or vegetable shortening, milk solids, sugar, an emulsifier, and flavorings. High-quality white chocolate contains a minimum of 32 percent cocoa butter.
6. **What are the differences between white chocolate couverture and white compound coating?**
White chocolate couverture contains a minimum of 32 percent cocoa butter and is of high quality. White compound coating, on the other hand, contains little or no cocoa butter. Instead, hydrogenated vegetable fat is used to replace all or most of the cocoa butter. Since solid vegetable fats have a higher melting point than cocoa butter and can leave a greasy feel on the tongue, they are viewed as being of lesser quality.
7. **In which dessert would tempering be necessary—a fudge brownie or chocolate-covered truffles?**
The chocolate used to dip the truffles would require tempering.
8. **What causes chocolate to seize?**
Chocolate seizes when it is exposed to very small quantities of water or exposed to humidity or steam. As chocolate is exposed to a drop or two of water, the cocoa solids within the chocolate clump together transforming it into a stiff, grainy mass.
9. **Name the three stages of tempering. Explain each one.**
The three stages of tempering are melting, cooling, and rewarming. The melting stage involves gently melting the chocolate over a double boiler to dissolve all the different types of fat crystals. The cooling stage involves cooling the chocolate down so that the beta fat crystals (the most stable, with the highest melting point) begin to recrystallize and take over. As the beta type of fat crystals begin to form, a chain reaction occurs in which the beta type multiply steadily. The rewarming stage involves getting the chocolate to a more liquid state by rewarming it to a specific temperature interval where the beta crystals are still solid. Once the temperature ranges of 86° to 91°F (30°–33°C) for semisweet and bittersweet chocolate and 86° to 89°F (30°–32°C) for milk and white chocolate are reached, the chocolate is said to be tempered as long as this interval is maintained during use. Tempered chocolate should dry in a short time and break with a snap when it does.
10. **Which method of tempering requires a clean, dry marble slab or stainless steel surface?**
The table method requires a clean, dry marble slab or stainless steel surface so a portion of the melted chocolate can be poured out and cooled by increasing its surface area. This happens during the cooling stage of tempering.

Test Questions

MULTIPLE CHOICE

1. After cocoa beans are roasted during the manufacturing of chocolate, what is removed after the beans are crushed?
   A. The chocolate liquor
   B. Theobroma cacao
   C. The nibs
   D. Cocoa solids

2. What is the melting point of cocoa butter?
   A. Human body temperature 98.6°F (37°C)
   B. Melting point is not relevant, since it is solid at most temperatures.
   C. Slightly below human body temperature 95°F (35°C)
   D. At 115°F (46°C) for milk chocolate and 120°F (49°C) for most semisweet chocolate

3. When cocoa powder has been treated with an alkali, it forms what product?
   A. Unsweetened cocoa powder
   B. Dutch processed cocoa powder
   C. Cocoa powder that has twice the acidity
   D. Cocoa powder with a chemical leavener added to it

4. What is the main reason why white chocolate is not a true chocolate?
   A. It contains no cocoa butter.
   B. It has a white, not dark color.
   C. It contains no chocolate liquor.
   D. It contains milk solids.

5. When is it necessary to temper chocolate?
   A. When the chocolate will be used within a recipe as an ingredient
   B. When the chocolate will be melted and shaped into a decoration on top of a cake
   C. When the chocolate will be used to coat candies such as truffles
   D. B and C

6. How should chocolate be properly melted?
   A. As quickly as possible to stabilize the fat crystals
   B. Gently over a double boiler
   C. In a container free of any moisture
   D. B and C

7. What are the three stages of tempering?
   A. Melting, cooling, and rewarming
   B. Melting, cooling, and remelting
   C. Melting, tabling, and scraping
   D. Seeding, melting, and rewarming

8. Which of the following phrases can be used to describe chocolate "bloom"?
   A. A whitish coating caused by fat crystals migrating to the surface of chocolate
   B. Bloom does not affect taste, only appearance.
   C. Dull streaks on chocolate caused by sugar crystals that are exposed to moisture and then resolidify on the surface of the chocolate
   D. All of the above

9. Common materials used to create molds for chocolate include which of the following?
   A. Tin
   B. Polycarbonate
   C. Thin plastic
   D. All of the above

10. Ganache is typically used to make which of the following desserts and confections?
    A. Rich chocolate frostings
    B. Truffles
    C. Chocolate cakes
    D. A and B

TRUE OR FALSE

11. _____ Chocolate liquor contains a minimum of 10 percent alcohol.

12. _____ Chocolate comes from the theochlora cacao tree, which grows in warm, tropical areas of the world.

13. _____ The more cocoa butter a chocolate contains, the higher its quality.

14. _____ Natural cocoa powder is acidic.

15. _____ Milk chocolate can be successfully substituted for any type of chocolate in baking.

16. _____ Couverture typically contains a larger quantity of cocoa butter.

17. _____ Tempering chocolate is a simple process that can be learned easily.

18. _____ When a drop of water mixes with chocolate and the chocolate clumps together, it is referred to as seizing.

19. _____ Of all the fat crystals present in chocolate, the beta type is the least stable.

20. _____ Compound coatings are used when tempering chocolate may be too time-consuming.

CHAPTER 20

Dessert Sauces and Plating

For video segments that correspond to this chapter, please see the About Professional Baking DVD series, Disk 3's chapter: *Dessert Sauces and Plating.*

Objectives

After reading this chapter, the student should be able to:

✓ Explain the four reasons to use dessert sauces.
✓ List the six basic types of dessert sauces.
✓ Use sauces to decorate a plate.
✓ Prepare the recipes in this chapter.

Key Terms

caramel

coulis

crème anglaise

custard sauce

dessert sauce

sabayon or zabaglione

Chapter Outline

I. Introduction—Dessert sauces are defined as a thickened liquid of some sort that is poured, drizzled, or piped onto a plate for decoration or directly onto food. They are to a pastry chef what paint is to an artist. This chapter discusses the four main reasons to use a dessert sauce, the six basic types of dessert sauces, and the art of decorating the dessert plate.

II. The Purpose of Dessert Sauces
   A. Add Moistness to Desserts
   B. Add Richness to Desserts
   C. Add Complementary Flavors to Desserts
   D. Create a More Attractive Presentation

III. Types of Dessert Sauces
   A. Uncooked Fruit Sauces
   B. Cooked Fruit Sauces Thickened with Starch
   C. Custard Sauces
      1. Crème Anglaise
      2. Sabayon
   D. Chocolate Sauces
   E. Caramel Sauce
   F. Reduction Sauce

IV. Painting a Plate with Sauces

V. How to Layer Different Sauces on One Plate
   A. Forming the Canvas
   B. Round Dots
   C. Hearts and Circle of Hearts
   D. Swirl Patterns
   E. Interweaving Lines
   F. Two-Tone Designs
   G. Looped Designs
   H. Painting the Bare Plate
   I. Coloring in Designs
   J. Drizzling Designs

VI. Tips to Follow When Painting Plates with Sauces

VII. Garnishes: Adding Depth and Dimension to a Dessert Plate

Review Questions and Answers

1. **Why are sauces so important to a pastry chef?**
   Sauces are important to a pastry chef because they can elevate a dessert to a higher level. Sauces act not only as a flavorful addition, they are also an artistic expression by the pastry chef.
2. **What are the four main reasons to use dessert sauces?**
   The four main reasons to use dessert sauces are to add moistness and richness to a dessert, add complementary flavors, and to create a more attractive presentation.
3. **Name the six basic types of dessert sauces.**
   The six basic types of dessert sauces are uncooked fruit sauces, cooked fruit sauces thickened with starch, custard sauces, chocolate sauces, caramel sauces, and reduction sauces.
4. **Describe the preparation of crème anglaise.**
   Crème anglaise is a stirred custard sauce containing egg yolks; sugar; milk, half-and-half, or heavy cream; and flavorings. The procedure to make crème anglaise begins with beating egg yolks and sugar until pale and light. Then hot milk, half-and-half, or heavy cream is whisked into the eggs to temper them. The mixture is then poured back into the saucepan which contained the milk or cream. The mixture is then cooked until a thermometer reads 180°F (82°C) and the mixture is thick enough to coat the back of a spoon. The custard is then poured through a strainer that has been placed into a bowl set over an ice bath. The strainer catches any lumps of egg protein and the ice bath immediately stops the cooking process. The mixture is then flavored, cooled, and chilled.

5. **How does a crème anglaise differ from a sabayon?**
   A crème anglaise is a French custard sauce that is prepared by whisking hot milk, half-and-half, or heavy cream into a beaten egg yolk and sugar mixture. A sabayon has a French and an Italian version. Egg yolks are whisked with sugar or a sugar syrup with no dairy products over a hot water bath until thickened. The Italian version adds wine to the mixture. While crème anglaise is typically used as a dessert sauce, a sabayon is generally either served on its own as a dessert or poured over fresh fruit.
6. **What is the simplest category of sauces?**
   The simplest of sauces includes the uncooked fruit sauce category. Ripened fruit is simply puréed and sweetened. The puréed ingredients are strained for a smoother sauce.
7. **Can starch-thickened fruit sauces be frozen?**
   It depends upon the type of starch that is used. Generally, most starch-thickened sauces cannot withstand freezing temperatures without breaking down.
8. **When decorating a plate with two or more sauces, why is it important for the sauces to be approximately the same thickness?**
   Designs will bleed into one another if the sauces are not of the same thickness or viscosity.
9. **Why is it important to make a test plate of the sauce design before plating the actual dessert?**
   By making a test plate before actually plating a sauce design, the chef can determine if the sauce is still of the same thickness and has not become too thick or too thin during refrigeration or storage.
10. **Describe how to form a spider web design using raspberry sauce and crème anglaise. A circle of hearts?**
    To form a spider web design using raspberry sauce and crème anglaise, one of the sauces is poured onto the center of the plate and spread so that the sauce evenly coats the bottom surface. Using a squirt bottle filled with the contrasting sauce, concentric circles are piped onto the base sauce. A skewer is then dragged from the center of the innermost circle and, moving outward through the remaining circles, towards the outer edge of the plate in a straight line. The skewer is then wiped clean and the above procedure is repeated but this time moving a short distance away from the first line. Again, this procedure is repeated completely around the plate spacing the drops evenly. To form a circle of hearts, one of the sauces is poured onto a plate to serve as a base and spread out evenly. Using the contrasting sauce in a squirt bottle, small dots are placed in a circle at a short distance from one another all around the plate. A wooden skewer is continuously drawn through the center of each dot in one direction starting from just above the first dot, forming a circle of hearts.

Test Questions

MULTIPLE CHOICE

1. What one of the reasons below is not a reason to use a dessert sauce?
   A. To add flavors to complement a dessert
   B. To add richness to a dessert
   C. To hide the flavor of a cake that did not come out as planned
   D. To add moistness to an otherwise dry desert
2. A sauce where ingredients are boiled on top of the stove to allow water to evaporate off so that the remaining liquid becomes concentrated is an example of what type of sauce?
   A. A cooked fruit sauce
   B. A reduction sauce
   C. A fruit coulis
   D. A custard sauce
3. Crème anglaise and sabayon are examples of which category of sauce?
   A. Custard
   B. Caramel
   C. Reduced
   D. Egg
4. If a cooked fruit sauce becomes too thick after cooling, what is generally added to thin it down?
   A. Water
   B. Milk
   C. A cornstarch and water mixture
   D. All of the above
5. You have just prepared a custard sauce. What is the main purpose of placing the custard sauce into a bowl set over an ice water bath?
   A. To thicken the custard
   B. To prevent bacterial growth
   C. To immediately stop the cooking process
   D. A and C
6. Which of the following liquids can be used to prepare a reduction sauce?
   A. Fruit juices
   B. Dairy liquid such as milk and heavy cream
   C. Wine
   D. A and C
7. Which of the following tools are used by pastry chefs to paint plates with sauce?
   A. Squirt bottles
   B. Parchment cones
   C. Wooden skewers or toothpicks
   D. All the above
8. To create plate designs using more than one sauce it is important that the sauces be similar in what way?
   A. Color
   B. Flavor components
   C. Consistency or density
   D. A and B
9. What type of plate would work best to highlight a sauce design with a raspberry sauce and crème anglaise?
   A. A plate with a design of flowers all over
   B. A solid-color plate that is light enough in color to contrast with the sauces
   C. A multi-striped plate
   D. Any color plate with any type of design would work
10. Which of the following is true of garnishes?
    A. They should be edible.
    B. They should add texture.
    C. They should add height.
    D. All of the above

TRUE OR FALSE

11. _____ An uncooked fruit sauce is one of the hardest sauces to make.
12. _____ Chocolate sauces very often are prepared from ganache.
13. _____ Custard sauces are not cooked.
14. _____ Simpler sauce designs are best when plating for a large crowd.
15. _____ A reduction sauce can be less fattening and caloric than a rich custard sauce.
16. _____ A test plate should be made to make sure all of the sauces to be used in a plate design are compatible in density.
17. _____ A dessert sauce is defined as a thin mixture that covers food.
18. _____ A typical coulis is made from a custard.
19. _____ Plated sauce designs can easily be seen on plates with patterns on them.
20. _____ A pool of raspberry sauce plated next to a chocolate tart provides a complementary flavor to the rich dessert.

CHAPTER 21
Healthy Baking

For video segments that correspond to this chapter, please see the About Professional Baking DVD series, Disk 2's chapter: *Healthy Baking.*

Objectives

After reading this chapter, the student should be able to:

✓ Modify some commonly used ingredients in recipes to healthier alternatives.

✓ Recognize the difference between more healthy and less healthy fats.

✓ List the three criteria for fat substitution.

✓ Identify the differences between sugar substitutes.

✓ Successfully substitute healthier ingredients for less healthy ingredients in recipes.

Key Terms

artificial sweeteners
saturated fats
unsaturated fats
trans-fats

Chapter Outline

I. Introduction—With a rise in obesity, heart disease, diabetes, and cancer the pastry chef must be sensitive to the needs of those consumers who have special dietary needs. This chapter discusses how to manipulate specific ingredients to modify recipes to create desserts that are healthier, have more nutritional value, and are just as delicious as the original version.

II. How to Modify Ingredients Containing Refined Grains with Healthier Alternatives to Enrich Baked Goods

III. Fats—Why They Are Necessary
   A. Saturated Fats
   B. Unsaturated Fats
      1. Trans-Fats
      2. Trans-Fat–Free Solid Margarines and Low-Fat Butters
      3. Fractionated Oils

IV. Substituting Healthier Fats for Less Healthy Fats
   A. The Role of Fat
   B. What Form the Fat Takes
   C. The Mixing Method Used

V. Some Healthier Fat Substitutions

VI. Replacing Sugar with Sugar Substitutes
   A. Saccharin
   B. Aspartame
   C. Sucralose
   D. Sugar Alcohols
      1. Maltitol

VII. Easy Substitutions

VIII. How to Modify a Recipe's Ingredients with Healthier Alternatives

IX. Antioxidants and Health

X. The Health Benefits of Chocolate

Review Questions and Answers

1. **Which fats are more healthy, the ones that are solid at room temperature or liquid at room temperature?**
In general, fats that are liquid at room temperature are healthier than those fats that are solid at room temperature because they tend to be unsaturated. Fats that are liquid at room temperature include oils such as canola and olive.

2. **Which liquid fats are unhealthy? Why?**
There are liquid fats known as tropical oils that originate from plants, which include coconut and palm kernel oils. They tend to be saturated. These fats are the exception to the general rule that states that fats that are liquid at room temperature will tend to be unsaturated and healthier. Saturated fats are associated with increasing the risk of obesity, cardiovascular disease, and certain types of cancers.

3. **Which is a healthier fat, monounsaturated or saturated? Why?**
Monounsaturated fats such as canola and olive oils tend to be healthier than saturated fats such as butter or lard. This is because monounsaturated fats tend to lower the bad cholesterol (low-density lipoprotein [LDL]) while saturated fats tend to raise it.

4. **Name three ways a baker could lower the amount of unhealthy fats in a cake recipe that uses butter and the creaming method.**
A cake recipe that uses butter and the creaming method of mixing requires a healthier fat substitute in a solid form for aeration. There are several ways to make an appropriate substitution. A low-fat, trans-fat–free butter or margarine would make a good substitute for the entire amount of fat in the original recipe. A second way would be to use half the amount of *regular* butter or margarine and half the amount of fat in the form of trans-fat–free butter or margarine. A third possibility would be to use half the amount of trans-fat–free butter or margarine and half the amount of applesauce or fruit purée. Some creaming with aeration will still occur if at least half of the fat is solid. This last substitution would yield the greatest decrease in the overall fat content of the recipe.
5. **Name the three key points of fat substitution.**
The three key points of fat substitution are looking at the role that the fat plays in the recipe, what form it takes, and the mixing method used.
6. **Name some healthy fat substitutes.**
Some healthy fat substitutions are replacing high-fat sour cream with a fat-free or low-fat version; replacing melted butter with canola oil, a monounsaturated fat; and replacing some of the butter with unsweetened applesauce.
7. **Name four sugar substitutes.**
Four sugar substitutes are saccharin, aspartame, sucralose, and maltitol.
8. **Why must you be careful in using a sugar substitute instead of sucrose in a cake recipe?**
Although all sugar substitutes have the ability to sweeten foods, they do not necessarily have the same chemical properties as real sugar (sucrose), making them difficult to use in certain types of recipes.
9. **Why can any sugar substitute be used to sweeten applesauce or a fruit filling?**
Any sugar substitute can be used to sweeten applesauce or a fruit filling because there are no specific baking properties that are needed to sweeten. If the sugar substitute was required to be a tenderizing or creaming agent for a recipe, the finished baked good may be less than satisfactory because the sugar substitute chosen did not have more of the same chemical properties as sucrose.
10. **How can grains other than white flour be used to boost the fiber and nutritional value of many baked goods?**
Many whole-grain flours, ground oats, nuts, and seeds can be used successfully in baked goods to boost fiber and nutritional value. Experimentation and taste are the best way to determine the correct amounts of modified ingredients needed to change from a refined grain to a more whole-grain ingredient. For example, start by replacing one fourth the amount of white flour in a recipe with an equal amount of whole wheat flour. Or, add ground oatmeal, wheat germ, or flax seed meal to most batters and doughs to improve texture and boost nutritional value.

Test Questions

MULTIPLE CHOICE

1. Why is white flour referred to as refined?
   A. Because vitamins and minerals have been added by the miller
   B. Because the outer part of the grain (the hull) was removed during processing
   C. Because the flour is very finely ground
   D. Because the flour is ground twice
2. Most saturated fats are derived from animals. Which of the following fats derived from plants are also saturated?
   A. Palm oil
   B. Lard
   C. Coconut oil
   D. A and C
3. Which of the following foods contains healthy omega–3 fatty acids?
   A. Chocolate mousse
   B. Walnuts
   C. Flax seeds
   D. B and C
4. Which of the following fats is the least healthy because it raises bad cholesterol (LDL's) and lowers good cholesterol (high-density lipoproteins [HDLs])?
   A. Monounsaturated
   B. Saturated
   C. Polyunsaturated
   D. Trans-fats
5. Which of the following is true of unsaturated fats?
   A. They are all solid at room temperature.
   B. They tend to be liquid at room temperature.
   C. They are derived from plants.
   D. B and C
6. If a recipe calls for melted butter, which of the following ingredients would make a healthier fat substitute yet not necessarily save on calories?
   A. Melted lard
   B. Fruit purée
   C. Canola oil
   D. Melted cocoa butter
7. You are preparing a pie crust with a low-fat trans-fat–free butter. What tips can you suggest to ensure the resulting crust will be flaky?
   A. Freeze the healthier fat for a short time to prevent it from melting too soon in the oven.
   B. Do not use a healthier substitute to prepare a flaky pie crust.
   C. Use some solid vegetable shortening for the flakiest crust.
   D. Roll the pastry thicker than you normally would.
8. Which of the following sugar substitutes contains no carbohydrates, provides little or no calories, and has no effect on blood sugar levels?
   A. Sucralose
   B. Sucrose
   C. Maltitol
   D. Galactose
9. Why does baking with certain sugar substitutes create baked goods that are so unsatisfactory in taste and texture?
   A. Most sugar substitutes provide zero calories.
   B. Some sugar substitutes are too sweet.
   C. All sugar substitutes are hygroscopic.
   D. Certain sugar substitutes do not have the same chemical properties as real sugar so baking with them can create problems.
10. What does the pastry chef need to keep in mind when modifying recipes to create baked goods that are more healthy?
    A. The modified healthier version of a baked good should be just as delicious as the original.
    B. Consumers are fickle and do not care about their health.
    C. Individual tastes paired with experimentation should be ignored by the pastry chef when modifying recipes.
    D. Pastry chefs cannot attempt to please everyone.

TRUE OR FALSE

11. _____ Replacing all the white flour in a recipe with whole wheat flour is a good start to making a recipe more healthy.

12. _____ Flax seed meal has been associated with increasing cardiovascular disease.

13. _____ Fats are important in baking and play many roles.

14. _____ All saturated fats are derived from animals.

15. _____ Knowing the mixing method that a recipe calls for will help to determine what type of healthier fat that can be substituted.

16. _____ Trans-fats are liquid fats that have undergone hydrogenation.

17. _____ Replacing high-fat ingredients with all fat-free ingredients will help to create not only a healthy baked good but also a delicious one.

18. _____ Maltitol is a good substitute for sugar since it behaves like sucrose.

19. _____ All sugar alcohols end in –OH.

20. _____ Fractionated oils are a poor alternative to hydrogenated oils.

CHAPTER 22
Troubleshooting

For video segments that correspond to this chapter, please see the About Professional Baking DVD series, where Chef Gail Sokol discusses common troubleshooting techniques she has mastered through years of experience.

Objectives

After reading this chapter, the student should be able to:

✓ Correct common mishaps or prevent them from happening the next time.

✓ Use common sense when baking, making sure to understand the methods, tools, and equipment needed.

Chapter Outline

I. Introduction—Mishaps in the bakeshop are common and are to be expected from time to time. Learning what went wrong with a particular recipe should be a learning experience to be applied the next time the recipe is made. This chapter was created as a reference to identify reasons why a baking mishap has occurred and the possible reasons that caused it. For the student's convenience, the order of each heading within this chapter corresponds with the chronologic order of how each chapter appears in the text.

II. What Can Go Wrong?
   - A. Directions Were Misread, Misinterpreted, or Not Followed Properly
   - B. Measuring of Ingredients Was Inaccurate
   - C. The Designated Mixing Method Was Not Followed
   - D. Inappropriate Ingredients Were Substituted for the Original
   - E. Flavorings Were Too Little or Too Much
   - F. The Wrong Size Pans Were Used
   - G. The Pans Were Not Prepped Properly
   - H. The Oven Was Not Working Properly
   - I. The Baked Good Did Not Come Out of the Pan

III. Custards

IV. Yeast Breads

V. Pies and Tarts

VI. Quick Breads

VII. Cakes

VIII. Frostings

IX. Cookies

X. Working with Sugar

XI. Frozen Desserts

XII. Chocolate

Review Questions and Answers

1. **If fudge frosting hardens too quickly, what can be done, if anything, to fix it?**
   If a fudge frosting hardens too quickly, it can be melted down over a double boiler or placed in a bowl set over a hot water bath. The frosting should then be cooled down until it is of a spreadable consistency.
2. **The pastry cream you made thickened nicely, but after it was left overnight in the refrigerator, it looked much thinner. Why?**
   Pastry creams are made from custards that contain egg yolks. Alpha-amylase, an enzyme in egg yolks, breaks down starches within a pastry cream unless it is destroyed during the cooking process. If the pastry cream did not come to a boil, the alpha-amylase will not be destroyed, and the mixture will thin out over several hours.
3. **What causes chocolate to seize and how can it be prevented?**
   Chocolate is very sensitive to moisture and humidity. Even a drop or two of moisture or water can cause chocolate to clump and seize. Gently whisking in a small amount of fat such as shortening or oil can help to smooth it out. Adding more water can also smooth the chocolate out but may disrupt the balance of the recipe. To prevent seizing, melt chocolate in a clean, dry saucepan over a double boiler or over a hot water bath, making sure to wipe the bottom of the bowl holding the chocolate before pouring it into other ingredients.
4. **What could be the cause of a skin forming over a custard?**
   A skin that forms on a custard is due to casein, a protein in milk, that forms a dry, crusty layer when exposed to air. Be sure to place plastic wrap, wax paper, or a layer of melted butter directly over the surface of the hot custard to prevent the surface from being exposed to air.
5. **What happens to a starch-thickened custard when it is overstirred?**
   A starch-thickened custard that has been overstirred will thin out because the starch granules begin to leak moisture back into the custard. Do not overstir custards and, once a custard has thickened, blend in flavorings gently.

6. **If you wanted cookies that spread out more as they baked, what ingredients might help?**
   To increase cookie spread, use a flour with less protein, more granulated sugar, and a fat with a lower melting point such as butter. More liquid can be added to the dough to thin it out, causing cookies to spread. Adding baking soda breaks down gluten and will cause cookies to spread.
7. **You added too much sugar to a sorbet base. What consequences might this have on the finished product?**
   Since sugar depresses the freezing point of water, preventing it from freezing to a rock-hard state, adding too much sugar will prevent the sorbet base from setting up and freezing to the proper consistency.
8. **The muffins you made had large holes throughout. What could have caused this?**
   Muffins with large holes or tunneling can be attributed to too much gluten formation. As the batter bakes, the thick network of gluten does not allow any trapped gases produced from the chemical leaveners to escape. These trapped gases explode within the muffins causing large holes to form. To prevent holes, mix ingredients just until combined.
9. **What caused a yeast bread to burst open during baking?**
   There could be many reasons why a yeast bread burst open during baking. One reason may be the oven was too hot or the bread was not slashed with a razor on top before baking. Other reasons may be that the dough was not shaped properly before baking; the dough was too dry and cracked open as it expanded; or the dough was overmixed, underfermented, or overfermented.
10. **When preparing a French buttercream, why should a boiling sugar syrup be added down the sides of the bowl and not directly onto the whip?**
    When preparing a French buttercream, the boiling sugar syrup should be added down the sides of the bowl and not directly onto the whip. This is because the syrup will form hard clumps if it hits the whip attachment and gets spun out onto the sides of the bowl.

Test Questions and Answers

MULTIPLE CHOICE

1. You overheated a stirred custard and notice there are some lumps. What, if anything, can you do to smooth the custard out?
   A. Nothing. The custard should be discarded.
   B. Process the stirred custard in a blender, then strain it to smooth it out.
   C. Add heavy cream and cook it again to smooth it out.
   D. Straining the custard and adding egg yolks will smooth it out while enriching it.
2. You work in a small commercial bakeshop and the cakes you have prepared seem overdone. What could be the cause and how should you rectify the situation?
   A. The oven might have been too hot; next time use an oven thermometer and place it on the middle rack in the middle of the oven to monitor the temperature so you can make adjustments to the setting.
   B. Too much baking powder was used. Next time omit it.
   C. Not enough sugar was added. Increase the sugar by one third next time.
   D. The batter had too much gluten. Next time use a low-protein flour.
3. After allowing egg yolks and granulated sugar to sit for a few minutes, you notice small lumps forming. What are these?
   A. The lumps are an egg emulsion beginning to form naturally.
   B. Since sugar is hydroscopic, it drew moisture from the egg.
   C. The egg proteins became dry and clumped together.
   D. B and C
4. A yeast bread you made crumbles apart and breaks. Which of the following reasons is not the one that could have caused this?
   A. The flour used had too little protein.
   B. Gluten was weak because not enough salt was used.
   C. Too much water was added to the dough.
   D. The dough was overproofed.
5. A pie crust you made was not flaky enough. What could have gone wrong?
   A. The fat was not cold enough and melted too quickly in the oven.
   B. A fat with too high a melting point was used.
   C. The water used was too cold.
   D. Too much gluten formed.
6. What could have caused a cake to overflow in the oven?
   A. Cake pans were overfilled.
   B. Cake pans were too small.
   C. Too much sugar was used.
   D. A and B
7. You wish to frost a cake with some newly made buttercream frosting but it is too thin. What should you do to get it to be of a spreadable consistency?
   A. Stir the buttercream over an icewater bath until it firms up and then beat it briefly to smooth it out.
   B. Place it in the freezer overnight to firm up.
   C. Add some frozen butter chunks to thicken it up.
   D. Throw it out and start over.
8. Your cookies spread out too much and were too thin. What can be done to prevent too much spread?
   A. Add more flour to the dough
   B. Replace some of the fat with shortening
   C. Chill the dough before baking
   D. All of the above
9. What could happen if a spoon was dipped into a boiling sugar syrup and then placed back into the mixture without being washed off?
   A. Sugar crystals on the spoon can cause the sugar syrup to suddenly solidify and crystallize.
   B. Nothing will happen.
   C. The sugar syrup will suddenly stop boiling.
   D. The sugar syrup will not crystallize as long as the spoon keeps stirring the mixture.
10. What could have prevented your sorbet base from freezing to the proper consistency?
    A. Too much sugar added to the base.
    B. The base was undercooked.
    C. Too much alcohol was added to the base.
    D. A and C

TRUE OR FALSE

11. ______ Using a small amount of cream of tartar can prevent a sugar syrup from crystallizing.
12. ______ Seizing never occurs with unsweetened chocolate.
13. ______ Cookies can become too dark when too much baking soda is added.
14. ______ Cold temperatures bring out flavors in frozen desserts so they do not need to be overly flavored.
15. ______ Directions for a recipe should be read carefully and thoroughly before beginning to bake.

16. _____ Overbeating ganache causes it to become hard and grainy.

17. _____ Eggs should be tempered when adding them to a hot liquid to prevent curdling.

18. _____ Substituting cake flour for bread flour in a recipe would work well.

19. _____ Properly tempering chocolate prevents fat bloom.

20. _____ A drop of water should not adversely affect melted chocolate.

Answers to Chapter Tests

Answers to Chapter 1 Test

Multiple Choice and True or False

1. D	8. A	15. T
2. C	9. D	16. F
3. A	10. A	17. T
4. D	11. C	18. T
5. B	12. F	19. F
6. D	13. F	20. T
7. C	14. F	21. T

Measurements

1. 2	10. 52	21. 4
2. $\frac{1}{2}$	11. 15	22. 8
3. 3	12. 8	23. 20
4. 32	13. 4	24. 5 pounds, 7 ounces
5. 3	14. volume	
6. 4	15. weight	25. 1000
7. 25 or 1 pound, 9 ounces	16. length	26. length
	17. weight	27. volume
	18. volume	28. weight
8. 1	19. 48	29. length
9. 1$\frac{1}{2}$	20. 128	30. volume

Baker's Percentages

1. Step A: Convert the bread flour from pounds and ounces to ounces (21 ounces).
   Step B: Multiply the weight of the flour by the percentage of each ingredient (in decimal form)

Raw wheat germ	21 × 0.1 = **2 ounces**
Instant active dry yeast	21 × 0.006 = 0.126 or **$\frac{1}{8}$ ounce**
Warm water	21 × 0.67 = **14 ounces**
Kosher salt	21 × 0.012 = 0.25 or **$\frac{1}{4}$ ounce**

2. Step A: Convert the new yield to ounces: 35 × 16 ounces/pound = **560 ounces.**
   Step B: Add up all the baker's percentages in the original recipe: 100% + 10% + 0.6% + 67% +1.2% = **178.8%.**
   Step C: Take this number and divide by 100 (this moves the decimal place two places to the left): 178.8/100 = 1.788 or, rounded, **1.79.**
   Step D: Divide step A by step C to get to the new amount of flour, set at 100%: 560 ounces/1 .79 = 312.8 or, rounded, **313 ounces.**
   Step E: Calculate the remaining ingredients based on the same percentages as the original by multiplying the new amount of flour and the percentages of each ingredient, rounding to the nearest 10th:

Bread flour	**313 ounces or 19$\frac{1}{2}$ pounds**	100%
Raw wheat germ	(313 × .1) = 31.3 or **31$\frac{1}{3}$ ounces**	10%
Instant active dry yeast	(313 × .006) = 1.8 or **2 ounces**	0.6%
Warm water	(313 × .67) = 209.7 or **210 ounces**	67%
Kosher salt	(313 × .012) = 3.76 or **4 ounces**	1.2%
	35 pounds	**178.8%**

Answers to Chapter 2 Test

1. D	8. D	15. T
2. D	9. A	16. F
3. A	10. D	17. T
4. B	11. T	18. T
5. B	12. F	19. T
6. B	13. T	20. T
7. B	14. F	

Answers to Chapter 3 Test

1. A	8. A	15. F
2. D	9. A	16. T
3. B	10. A	17. T
4. C	11. T	18. T
5. A	12. T	19. F
6. C	13. F	20. T
7. B	14. F	

Answers to Chapter 4 Test

1. B	8. B	15. F
2. C	9. C	16. T
3. C	10. A	17. T
4. A	11. F	18. F
5. D	12. T	19. F
6. C	13. T	20. F
7. B	14. T	

Answers to Chapter 5 Test

1. C	8. B	15. T
2. A	9. C	16. F
3. B	10. D	17. T
4. B	11. T	18. T
5. A	12. T	19. F
6. B	13. F	20. T
7. B	14. F	

Answers to Chapter 6 Test

1. A	8. A	15. F
2. C	9. C	16. F
3. D	10. D	17. T
4. B	11. F	18. F
5. A	12. T	19. T
6. B	13. T	20. T
7. B	14. T	

Answers to Chapter 7 Test

1. D	8. A	15. F
2. A	9. B	16. T
3. B	10. D	17. T
4. B	11. T	18. T
5. D	12. F	19. T
6. A	13. F	20. F
7. C	14. T	

Answers to Chapter 8 Test

1. A	8. B	15. T
2. D	9. A	16. F
3. B	10. A	17. T
4. C	11. F	18. F
5. A	12. T	19. F
6. D	13. T	20. T
7. B	14. F	

Answers to Chapter 9 Test

1. D	8. D	15. F
2. B	9. B	16. F
3. A	10. A	17. F
4. D	11. T	18. F
5. B	12. F	19. T
6. D	13. T	20. T
7. A	14. T	

Answers to Chapter 10 Test

1. D	8. A	15. F
2. B	9. B	16. T
3. B	10. C	17. T
4. D	11. F	18. T
5. A	12. T	19. F
6. B	13. F	20. T
7. C	14. F	

Answers to Chapter 11 Test

1. B	8. D	15. T
2. A	9. A	16. F
3. D	10. B	17. T
4. D	11. T	18. T
5. B	12. F	19. F
6. B	13. T	20. T
7. B	14. T	

Answers to Chapter 12 Test

1. B	8. B	15. T
2. D	9. A	16. F
3. D	10. A	17. T
4. B	11. T	18. F
5. B	12. F	19. T
6. A	13. F	20. F
7. D	14. F	

Answers to Chapter 13 Test

1. A	8. D	15. F
2. D	9. B	16. F
3. B	10. D	17. T
4. D	11. F	18. F
5. D	12. F	19. T
6. C	13. F	20. F
7. C	14. T	

Answers to Chapter 14 Test

1. D	8. C	15. T
2. D	9. D	16. F
3. B	10. A	17. F
4. C	11. T	18. T
5. A	12. T	19. T
6. D	13. T	20. F
7. A	14. F	

Answers to Chapter 15 Test

1. D	8. B	15. T
2. B	9. B	16. T
3. D	10. B	17. T
4. D	11. T	18. F
5. B	12. F	19. F
6. B	13. F	20. T
7. D	14. F	

Answers to Chapter 16 Test

1. C	8. B	15. F
2. B	9. C	16. F
3. C	10. C	17. F
4. D	11. F	18. T
5. D	12. T	19. T
6. D	13. T	20. T
7. A	14. F	

Answers to Chapter 17 Test

1. B	8. C	15. T
2. A	9. D	16. T
3. B	10. C	17. F
4. D	11. T	18. T
5. D	12. T	19. F
6. C	13. F	20. T
7. D	14. F	

Answers to Chapter 18 Test

1. A	8. D	15. F
2. B	9. B	16. T
3. D	10. B	17. F
4. D	11. T	18. T
5. A	12. F	19. T
6. C	13. T	20. F
7. A	14. F	

Answers to Chapter 19 Test

1. C	8. D	15. F
2. C	9. D	16. T
3. B	10. D	17. F
4. C	11. F	18. T
5. D	12. F	19. F
6. D	13. T	20. T
7. A	14. T	

Answers to Chapter 20 Test

1. C	8. C	15. T
2. B	9. B	16. T
3. A	10. D	17. F
4. A	11. F	18. F
5. C	12. T	19. F
6. D	13. F	20. T
7. D	14. T	

Answers to Chapter 21 Test

1. B
2. D
3. D
4. D
5. D
6. C
7. A
8. A
9. D
10. A
11. F
12. F
13. T
14. F
15. T
16. T
17. F
18. T
19. T
20. F

Answers to Chapter 22 Test

1. B
2. A
3. D
4. C
5. A
6. D
7. A
8. D
9. A
10. D
11. T
12. F
13. T
14. F
15. F
16. T
17. T
18. F
19. T
20. F

Answers to the About Professional Baking Student Workbook

Student Workbook Chapter 1

EXPLAIN THESE KEY TERMS

1. A system used by professional bakers in large commercial operations that involves percentages to express formulas in a simple way.
2. To fix or correct the measurement standards on a scale or other measuring device.
3. The term used by professional bakers for a recipe.
4. The level of free flowing liquid in a measuring container that marks the amount of the liquid the container is holding.
5. A French term meaning "getting everything ready and in its place" to help a chef get organized by putting all ingredients together to get ready to bake.
6. The act of weighing ingredients.
7. The temperature range between 41°F (5°C)–135°F (57°C) in which bacteria grow very quickly in foods.

FILL IN THE BLANKS

8. practicing good sanitation
9. mise en place
10. formulas
11. mixing method
12. scaling
13. pathogens
14. Salmonella
15. metric
16. baker's scale
17. liquid measuring cups; solid measuring cups
18. tare
19. flour
20. Bain marie

TRUE OR FALSE

21. F
22. F
23. T
24. T
25. F
26. T
27. T
28. F
29. F
30. T

MULTIPLE CHOICE

31. A
32. C
33. B
34. C
35. A
36. B
37. A
38. B
39. A
40. C

MATCH THE FOLLOWING

41. H
42. G
43. I
44. F
45. A
46. B
47. C
48. D
49. E
50. J

Student Workbook Chapter 2

EXPLAIN THESE KEY TERMS

1. Ingredients that are usually in particle form like flour, sugar, baking soda, etc.
2. A process where fat blobs are broken down into tiny particles so that they stay evenly dispersed in milk.
3. The procedure where a food substance is heated to a specific temperature for a specific time in order to kill dangerous microorganisms that can cause foodborne illness.
4. The ability of a fat to hold its solid shape at room temperature while still having the ability to be molded
5. Non liquids that hold their shape such as butter, cream cheese, etc.
6. When milk or cream is held at an even higher temperature (280°–300°F or 138°–150° C) than in pasteurization. The product has a longer shelf life but the cream will not attain the same volume when whipped.
7. Ingredients that can be poured.

FILL IN THE BLANKS

8. hard/soft; soft/hard
9. carbohydrates
10. starches
11. Gelatins
12. fats
13. melting point
14. Canola
15. fat
16. ½% to 3%
17. essential oils
18. processed flavorings
19. kosher
20. sugar

TRUE OR FALSE

21. F
22. T
23. F
24. T
25. F
26. T
27. T
28. T
29. T
30. T

MULTIPLE CHOICE

31. B
32. A
33. C
34. C
35. C
36. A
37. A
38. B
39. A
40. A

MATCH THE FOLLOWING

41. F
42. A
43. B
44. C
45. D
46. E
47. G
48. J
49. I
50. H

Student Workbook Chapter 3

EXPLAIN THESE KEY TERMS

1. Flour made from a combination of hard and soft wheats suited for all purposes.
2. Exposes the newly milled flour to chlorine gas or benzoyl peroxide to remove the pale yellow color and improve the gluten quality.
3. The general term for flour that is milled from wheat having a higher protein content and used for bread making.
4. Whole wheat kernels are passed through two steel rollers to separate the endosperm, bran, and germ.
5. A flour milled from soft wheats that is typically bleached and used for only the most tender cakes and pastries.
6. The final stage of flour milling where the same size particles of flour are categorized.
7. The particles of flour from the outermost layers of the endosperm. It is the flour that remains after patent flour is removed.
8. One of the two proteins in gluten.
9. A network of fibers that is created when the two proteins in wheat are mixed with water. This web of fibers keeps gases trapped causing baked goods to rise.
10. One of the two proteins in gluten.
11. A flour made from soft wheats containing more starch than protein.
12. The finest particles of flour taken from the inner part of the endosperm.
13. Removing any remnants of bran from the endosperm after breaking the wheat.
14. Part of the milling process where endosperm are ground into flour.
15. Part of the milling process where particles of flour are sorted by size.
16. Particles of milled flour that are sorted by size in order to be classified.

FILL IN THE BLANKS

17. bran
18. smallest
19. endosperm
20. pastry/cake; cake/pastry
21. 14%; 6-8%
22. wheat berry
23. Patent
24. germ
25. durum

TRUE OR FALSE

26. F
27. F
28. T
29. F
30. F
31. T
32. T
33. F
34. T
35. F

MULTIPLE CHOICE

36. C
37. C
38. A
39. A
40. B

MATCH THE FOLLOWING

41. B
42. A
43. I
44. J
45. C
46. H
47. G
48. F
49. E
50. D

Student Workbook Chapter 4

EXPLAIN THESE KEY TERMS

1. An attachment for electric mixers that simulates kneading bread dough.
2. A group of ingredients including butter, oils, lard, margarine, and vegetable shortening.
3. A very gentle method of blending lighter, air-filled ingredients into heavier batters without losing air volume.
4. A bowl with a blade inside it attached to an electric motor that is used for chopping and blending.
5. A network of fibers that is created when the two proteins in wheat are mixed with water. This web of fibers keeps gases trapped causing baked goods to rise and provide strength and structure.
6. When different ingredients are thoroughly mixed together to form a uniformly blended mixture.
7. A mixing tool used on an electric mixer shaped like a boat's oar with open spaces in between.
8. A tool consisting of five or six bent metal wires attached to a handle used to cut fat into flour.
9. A tool consisting of a soft, rubber, scoop-like spoon attached to a wooden, plastic, or metal handle that is used to gently blend or fold ingredients.
10. An attachment for electric mixers shaped like a whisk that beats air into ingredients.
11. Looped metal wires attached to a handle.

FILL IN THE BLANKS

12. liquid
13. lightness
14. toughness
15. rubber spatula
16. friction
17. more; less
18. leavening
19. carbon dioxide
20. folding

TRUE OR FALSE

21. T
22. F
23. F
24. T
25. F
26. T
27. T
28. F
29. T
30. F

MULTIPLE CHOICE

31. A
32. C
33. C
34. B
35. A

MATCH THE FOLLOWING

36. C
37. A
38. B
39. D
40. E
41. I
42. G
43. J
44. H
45. F

Student Workbook Chapter 5

EXPLAIN THESE KEY TERMS

1. An enzyme in raw egg yolks that breaks down starches.
2. Addition of cold water to gelatin causing it to absorb the liquid so it appears to be blooming.
3. A type of seaweed from Ireland that is similar to agar that is used to thicken foods containing dairy products.
4. A stabilizer that helps foods to form a gel like consistency giving structure to desserts.
5. The process that starch granules go through to ultimately thicken a liquid.
6. When gelatin firms up or sets up to become a solid-like gel.
7. It comes from the sticky sap of an African tree and is useful in stabilizing emulsions in frostings and fillings.
8. A gum derived from a Middle Eastern shrub it is used for gum paste decorations and flowers and as a stabilizer when it is mixed into fondant.
9. The collective term for gelatin that is derived from plants, also known as vegetable gums.
10. A type of thickener made from the natural sugars in cell walls of plants. Located in unripened fruits it is used to thicken jellies, jams, preserves, and glazes.
11. Long chain of sugars chemically bonded to one another in the form of semi crystalline shapes. Used to thicken desserts like pastry cream and pie fillings.

FILL IN THE BLANKS

12. amylopectin
13. thickening
14. modified starches
15. thickening of the liquid
16. thin
17. gluten
18. protein
19. sheets
20. gelatin

TRUE OR FALSE

21. F
22. T
23. T
24. F
25. F
26. T
27. F
28. T
29. F
30. T

MULTIPLE CHOICE

31. A
32. B
33. B
34. A
35. A

MATCH THE FOLLOWING

36. G
37. H
38. J
39. F
40. E
41. D
42. C
43. B
44. A
45. I

Student Workbook Chapter 6

EXPLAIN THESE KEY TERMS

1. A pocket of air at the larger end of the egg.
2. An enzyme found in raw eggs that feeds on starch causing it to break down.
3. The building blocks of proteins.
4. A French term for a warm water bath that can either be used to warm or melt ingredients.
5. A mixture of eggs and milk or cream, sometimes with additional ingredients, which is poured into a container and baked in the oven until thickened.
6. The process in which cooking continues for a short period of time, even though the heat source has been removed.
7. A protein in milk and other dairy products which, when exposed to air, forms a crusty skin.
8. When proteins are heated and moisture gets trapped in between each protein coil, forming a protein network producing a thick, gel-like structure as when a custard thickens.
9. When egg proteins clump together because they are heated for too long and at too high a temperature.
10. A sweet, French stirred custard sauce used as a dessert sauce or as a base for frozen desserts. A typical crème anglaise is flavored with vanilla and is referred to as a vanilla sauce.
11. When proteins, like eggs, are heated, beaten, or acidified, causing the protein strands or coils to straighten out or break apart.
12. A protein that speeds up a chemical reaction.
13. The procedure where a food substance is heated to a specific temperature for a specific amount of time in order to kill dangerous microorganisms that can cause foodbourne illness.
14. A stirred custard consisting of eggs, milk, sugar, and a starch such as flour or cornstarch that is used as a filling for cream pies, fruit tarts, and cream puffs.
15. When a membrane or surface allows air or moisture through it. An eggshell is porous allowing odors in and moisture to evaporate out.
16. Chains or strands of amino acids chemically linked together.
17. To heat a liquid to just below the boiling point.
18. A mixture of eggs and milk or cream stirred on top of the stove with or without the addition of a starch and cooked until thickened.
19. Slowing adding a hot mixture into a cold mixture containing eggs to prevent the mixture from coagulating.
20. Foods that help ingredients to become less fluid and more dense.

FILL IN THE BLANKS

21. 2 oz.
22. 4-5 weeks
23. chalazae
24. air cell
25. jumbo; large
26. liquid whole egg substitutes
27. thickeners
28. custard
29. Pastry cream
30. stirred/baked; baked/stirred

TRUE OR FALSE

31. F
32. T
33. T
34. T
35. F
36. T
37. T
38. F
39. T
40. T

MULTIPLE CHOICE

41. A
42. B
43. A
44. C
45. A

MATCH THE FOLLOWING

46. J
47. G
48. D
49. C
50. F
51. B
52. E
53. I
54. H
55. A

Student Workbook Chapter 7

EXPLAIN THESE KEY TERMS

1. An acidic by-product of wine making used to help denature the egg protein. Also called potassium hydrogen tartrate.
2. Eggs with air beaten in by a whisk.
3. Uncooked mixture of beaten egg whites and sugar.
4. The property of sugar when it absorbs moisture.
5. Egg whites beaten with the addition of sugar that has been boiled to 240°–250°F (115°–122°C).
6. A light foamy confection made from Italian meringue that is stabilized with gelatin.
7. Mixtures of beaten egg whites and sugar, usually with the addition of an acid such as cream of tartar or lemon juice.
8. The procedure where a food substance is heated at a specific temperature for a specific amount of time in order to kill dangerous microorganisms that can cause food borne illness.
9. A bacteria associated with eggs that can cause foodborne illness.
10. The stage of beating meringue until the beater is held up and the meringue curls over itself.
11. A light airy food usually consisting of three parts—custard, flavoring, and beaten egg whites.
12. The stage of beating a meringue when the beater is held up and the meringue stands straight up in a vertical peak.
13. Eggs and sugar warmed to 140°F (60°C) over an egg bath and then beaten to peaks.

FILL IN THE BLANKS

14. air; proteins
15. denatures
16. meringues
17. Soft
18. three
19. expands
20. leavening agent
21. egg foams
22. an Italian

TRUE OR FALSE

23. F
24. T
25. T
26. T
27. F
28. T
29. F
30. T
31. F
32. T

MULTIPLE CHOICE

33. C
34. A
35. A
36. A
37. C
38. C
39. A
40. C
41. A
42. C

MATCH THE FOLLOWING

43. F
44. B
45. E
46. A
47. C
48. D
49. G
50. I
51. J
52. G

Student Workbook Chapter 8

EXPLAIN THESE KEY TERMS

1. Dehydrated yeast sold in granulated form.
2. The resting period after mixing flour and water.
3. The act of placing food such as a dough or other unbaked pastry in the oven where dry heat cooks the food.
4. A piece of heavy canvas or linen in which a yeast bread can be nestled in order to hold its shape during the proofing process.
5. The same as punching. A stage in yeast bread baking where, after the dough has fermented, the edges of the dough are pulled over into the center to deflate it releasing carbon dioxide and redistributing the yeast.
6. In bread baking, the first rise of a yeast dough where carbon dioxide gases become trapped in a network of gluten.
7. Fresh yeast mixed with a starch that is portioned into a small cube.
8. The difference between the temperature of the dough before and after mixing.
9. During the baking process starches within flour absorb moisture from the dough, swell, and become firm.
10. A protein fragment—amino acid—found in active dry yeast that weakens gluten in yeast doughs.
11. A network of fibers that is created when the two proteins in wheat are mixed with water. This web of fibers keeps gases trapped causing baked goods to rise and provide strength and structure.
12. Similar to active dry yeast but with fewer dead yeast cells. Contains ascorbic acid.
13. A stage in yeast bread making where the dough is pushed against a work surface and folded over on itself until a smooth, elastic dough has developed. Gluten is developed during this process.
14. A yeast dough that does not contain fat or sugar.
15. An ingredient that is added to baked goods to help them rise.
16. A reaction between amino acids and sugars that occurs between 300°F(149°C) and 500°F(260 °C) causing the outer crust of breads to caramelize and brown.
17. The act of combining ingredients.
18. A variation of the straight dough method for mixing yeast breads where the fat and the sugar are combined before being added to the other ingredients to ensure their even distribution.
19. The tendency of water to go from a higher concentration of itself through a permeable membrane to a lower concentration of itself in an attempt to balance the concentrations and form an equilibrium.
20. A yeast used in rich sweet doughs that contain greater amounts of sugar, fats, and eggs. Osmotolerant yeast is able to rehydrate without large amounts of water present in the dough and without being damaged due to its tolerance of osmotic changes within a dough.
21. The rapid rising of a yeast dough in the oven due to trapped gases within the dough that are expanding.
22. Rehydrating yeast by mixing in warm water or letting the dough rise in a warm controlled environment.
23. An enzyme naturally occurring in dairy products that breaks down proteins and can have a negative effect on gluten formation in yeast doughs.
24. A stage in yeast bread baking where after the dough is scaled and rounded it is covered and allowed to relax for a short period of time. This allows gluten to relax before shaping.
25. A yeast dough that contains greater amounts of fat and sugar. It may also contain eggs. Examples are brioche, coffee cakes, and cinnamon rolls.
26. The act of weighing ingredients.
27. Making shallow cuts with a razor on the surface of an unbaked loaf of yeast bread to allow the bread to expand during baking.
28. A stage in the yeast bread baking process when scaled pieces of dough are formed into the desired shapes that will be placed in the oven.
29. A method of yeast dough preparation in which the dough is prepared in two stages. First a portion of the flour, water, and yeast are mixed together and allowed to ferment then the other ingredients are added.
30. A yeast dough in which most of the ingredients are mixed together in one bowl.
31. The simplest mixing methods for yeast breads where all ingredients are mixed together in one bowl.
32. A liquid used to brush over food before baking such as a yeast dough to add color, shine or help toppings to adhere.
33. A one celled microscopic living fungus that undergoes fermentation and is used as a leavening agent for yeast breads and in the production of cheese, beer, and wine.

FILL IN THE BLANKS

34. gas
35. Straight
36. yeast
37. moisture/warmth/sugar; warmth/sugar/moisture; moisture/warmth/sugar;
38. one year
39. Proofing
40. 5 – 10 minutes

TRUE OR FALSE

41. F
42. T
43. F
44. T
45. F
46. T
47. F
48. F
49. T
50. F

MULTIPLE CHOICE

51. A
52. B
53. C
54. B
55. C

MATCH THE FOLLOWING

56. D
57. A
58. B
59. C
60. H
61. I
62. G
63. J
64. F
65. E

Student Workbook Chapter 9

EXPLAIN THESE KEY TERMS

1. One of two species of bacteria found in sourdough.
2. Breads that are prepared by bakers that manipulate the dough with their hands with great care and skill using traditional methods.
3. An Italian preferment.
4. The beginning stages of a sourdough starter.
5. The heat energy transferred to a yeast dough through the act of mixing.
6. A bacteria that exists in sourdough.
7. A sourdough starter made from wild yeast that is used to leaven sourdough bread known as pain du Levain.
8. A preferment using commercial yeast.
9. A starter that uses wild yeast that is present in the air or on fruits or vegetables.
10. French for Polish, it refers to a thin sponge starter typically prepared with equal parts of flour and water by weight.
11. Meaning to ferment before it is a mixture of flour, water, and yeast that is allowed to ferment before the actual dough is made.
12. A term referring to a slowing down of the fermentation process by placing the dough in a special temperature controlled box called a retarder or in the refrigerator for several hours.
13. A type of preferment that uses natural or wild yeast.
14. A culture or starter that uses wild or natural yeast containing bacteria that produce flavorful acids.

FILL IN THE BLANKS

15. altus brat
16. commercial
17. 50-60%
18. longer/more; less
19. old dough
20. acetobacillus
21. chef
22. bacteria
23. carbon dioxide
24. in one bowl
25. preferments

TRUE OR FALSE

26. F
27. T
28. T
29. T
30. T
31. T
32. F
33. F
34. F
35. F

MULTIPLE CHOICE

36. A
37. B
38. C
39. B
40. B

MATCH THE FOLLOWING

41. E
42. D
43. B
44. C
45. F
46. G
47. H
48. I
49. J
50. A

Student Workbook Chapter 10

EXPLAIN THESE KEY TERMS

1. The dough in which the fat is wrapped when making laminated doughs.
2. Method of rolling dough into a rectangle and folding the ends to the middle and bring the two halves together as in a book.
3. Also known as and another word for base dough.
4. Rich doughs with or without yeast in which fat has been incorporated through a series of folds or turns which, when baked, form hundreds of layers of flaky pastry.
5. Physical property of fats referring to how easily it can be shaped or shaped dependent on the temperature surrounding it.
6. When laminated dough is folded into thirds like a letter to incorporate the fat.
7. The sequence of rolling and folding out the laminated dough.

FILL IN THE BLANKS

8. sugar
9. rectangle
10. enclosing the fat
11. rest; one hour
12. sweet/savory; savory/sweet
13. three
14. four
15. layers; rise
16. type of fat
17. They are less expensive
18. shortenings
19. 60 degrees F; 16 degrees C

TRUE OR FALSE

20. F
21. T
22. F
23. T
24. T
25. F
26. T
27. F
28. T
29. T

MULTIPLE CHOICE

30. C
31. C
32. A
33. B
34. B
35. B
36. B
37. B
38. A

MATCH THE FOLLOWING

39. B
40. A
41. D
42. C
43. K
44. E
45. F
46. G
47. I
48. J
49. H

Student Workbook Chapter 11

EXPLAIN THESE KEY TERMS

1. Baking an unfilled pie or pastry shell.
2. Piercing the pie or pastry dough on the bottom and sides to prevent puffing during baking.
3. A free form tart filled with fruit.
4. It means "broken pastry" in French for its flaky quality when baked. It is one of three types of pastry crusts.
5. One of three types of pastry crusts it means "sandy pastry" in French its crumbly quality when baked. This sweet short dough cannot be rolled but must be pressed into a pan or form.
6. One of three types of pastry crusts it means "sweet" or "sugar" pastry in French. This short, sweet dough can be rolled for pie or tart crusts.
7. Like docking, it is the method for piercing the dough on the bottom and sides prior to baking to prevent puffing.

FILL IN THE BLANKS

8. pâté brisée
9. tart
10. gluten, shortening
11. spacers
12. flaky; mealy
13. cold
14. butter
15. acid
16. gluten
17. blind baking
18. water
19. puffing
20. refrigerated
21. shrinkage

TRUE OR FALSE

22. T
23. T
24. T
25. T
26. F
27. F
28. T
29. T

MULTIPLE CHOICE

30. B
31. A
32. B
33. A
34. B
35. C
36. A
37. B
38. C

MATCH THE FOLLOWING

39. D
40. E
41. A
42. F
43. B
44. C
45. G

Student Workbook Chapter 12

EXPLAIN THESE KEY TERMS

1. A chemical leavener which in the presence of moisture and heat produces ammonia, carbon dioxide, and water. All three of these byproducts can act as leaveners.
2. A chemical leavener including baking soda or sodium bicarbonate and at least acid that is used to help baked goods rise.
3. A chemical leavener also known as sodium bicarbonate or bicarbonate that when it combines with an acid in the presence of moisture is used to help baked goods rise.
4. Chemical substances that help the mixed ingredients rise in the oven such as baking soda, baking powder, and ammonium carbonate.
5. One of two types of baking powder it reacts twice, once to moisture and secondly to heat.
6. A versatile steam leavened dough used for cream puffs, éclairs, and other filled pastries.
7. A chemical reaction between equal amounts of an acid and a base that results in the formation of a salt and water. This results in a neutral pH of 7.0.
8. This is the same as éclair paste and choux paste. In French it means cabbage paste because of the shape of a finished cream puff.
9. A puffy quick bread with a brown exterior and eggy center.
10. A category of breads that are leavened with carbon dioxide gas from chemical leaveners and are quick to prepare.
11. A combination of baking soda and cream of tartar that needs only water to react and is very fast acting. It is seldom used.
12. The result of heating water to 212 degrees F. Can be used as the sole leavener or in combination with yeast and chemical leaveners.

FILL IN THE BLANKS

13. chemical
14. baking soda/bicarbonate of soda/sodium bicarbonate
15. double-acting
16. steam
17. neutralization
18. acids/bases; bases/acids
19. Acids; bases
20. acids
21. air
22. profiteroles
23. whole eggs

TRUE OR FALSE

24. F
25. F
26. T
27. T
28. F
29. F
30. F
31. T
32. F
33. F
34. T

MULTIPLE CHOICE

35. B
36. C
37. A
38. A
39. C
40. B
41. C
42. A
43. B
44. A

MATCH THE FOLLOWING

45. D
46. B
47. A
48. E
49. C
50. F

Student Workbook Chapter 13

EXPLAIN THESE KEY TERMS

1. A mixing method for quick breads that resembles the method for pâte brisée or flaky pie crust consisting of first cutting cold fat into dry ingredients followed by the addition of the liquid ingredients.
2. A method of mixing granulated or brown sugar with a softened, solid fat until light and fluffy.
3. A method of mixing quick bread where granulated or brown sugar is mixed with a softened, solid fat using the paddle attachment of an electric mixer until it is light and fluffy.
4. The method of mixing fat with dry ingredients.
5. A quick bread mixing method consists of dry ingredients being mixed into a bowl of liquid ingredients.
6. A puffy quick bread with a brown exterior and a hollow eggy center that uses steam as a leavening agent.
7. Large holes or cavities throughout the inside of a baked item that can be caused by overmixing.

FILL IN THE BLANK

8. creaming
9. overmixed
10. yeast
11. temperature
12. during
13. gluten
14. biscuit
15. muffin
16. fat/shortening
17. liquid
18. sugar/fat; fat/sugar
19. cutting
20. two-thirds
21. tunneling

TRUE OR FALSE

22. F
23. F
24. T
25. F
26. F
27. T
28. T
29. T
30. F
31. F

MULTIPLE CHOICE

32. A
33. A
34. C
35. B
36. B
37. C
38. B
39. B
40. B
41. C

MATCH THE FOLLOWING

42. D
43. I
44. F
45. H
46. A
47. B
48. E
49. C
50. G
51. J

Student Workbook Chapter 14

EXPLAIN THESE KEY TERMS

1. A cake mixing method for cakes low in fats.
2. Cakes that rely on solid and liquid fats to keep gluten development low.
3. Cakes that rely on ingredients other than fat to tenderize them, such as sugar.
4. A mixing method for cakes low in fat that usually uses a liquid fat, such as oil, and a chemical leavener.
5. A mixing method for cakes high in fat in which the fat and sugar are mixed until fluffy.
6. The type of low fat cake that uses beaten eggs to leaven them.
7. A uniform mixture of two unmixable substances, such as fat and water, that create a homogeneous mixture that will not separate out.
8. A food, like egg yolks, or an additive that allows two immiscible liquids to stay uniformed.
9. A cake that contains more sugar than flour by weight.
10. Two unmixable liquids that do not ordinarily stay mixed together, such as oil and water.
11. The simplest mixing method for cakes high in fat in which all ingredients are added in one bowl.
12. A mixing method for cakes low in fat where eggs are used as the leavening agent.
13. A mixing method for cakes high in fat where liquids are added in two stages.

FILL IN THE BLANKS

14. high/low; low/high
15. two-stage method
16. sponge method
17. high ratio cake
18. oil
19. separated egg foams
20. genoise

TRUE OR FALSE

21. T
22. T
23. F
24. T
25. F
26. F
27. F
28. T
29. T
30. F

MULTIPLE CHOICE

31. A
32. C
33. A
34. B
35. C
36. C
37. C
38. B
39. A
40. C

MATCH THE FOLLOWING

41. C
42. J
43. A
44. B
45. H
46. F
47. D
48. E
49. I
50. G

Student Workbook Chapter 15

EXPLAIN THESE KEY TERMS

1. A clear thin plastic used in protecting the sides of cakes, or coating the sides of cakes with chocolate.
2. A frosting consisting of butter or vegetable shortening, granulated sugar, corn syrup, or confectioners' sugar, and whole eggs, yolks or whites.
3. Two types of chocolate frosting based on two types of chocolate confections—fudge and truffles.
4. Italian or Swiss meringues to which gelatin may be added.
5. A sweet topping or covering used to fill and/or coat a cake, cookie or other pastry.
6. A mixture of cream, chocolate, and flavorings which can be used for frostings, glazes, sauces, and candies.
7. A rectangular or triangular piece of hard plastic or metal in which grooves or ridges have been cut at regular intervals. Dragged along the sides and tops of newly frosted cakes it leaves a design.
8. A stainless steel circular strip like pan with no top or bottom. Used to mold layers of cake with fillings and also as a cake pan when placed on aluminum foil on a sheet pan.
9. A metal bottom that is slid between the cake layers to help remove the top layer.
10. A palette knife having a slight bend in the blade just before the handle.
11. A narrow metal spatula.
12. A cone shaped hollow bag made of various materials that can be filled with frostings, batters, doughs or chocolate. When squeezed the bag forces the filling through a tip at the narrow end that makes decorative shapes.
13. A brush resembling a paintbrush used to apply glazes, butter, water or egg washes.
14. A hollow metal cone shape with varying cuts at the smaller end that is fitted into a pastry bag.
15. Frosting with the consistency of a dough that may be made of various ingredients such as fondant, modeling chocolate, or marzipan.
16. A fluffy uncooked decorative icing made of confectioner's sugar, an acid such as lemon juice or cream of tartar, and egg whites. Resembles a meringue that dries very hard and used to create piped decorations or flowers on cakes.
17. An easy icing made of confectioner's sugar sand water, with cream, milk, citrus juices, or corn syrup to which other flavors are added. It is a thin pourable icing.
18. A rotating elevated plate used to facilitate frosting a cake.

FILL IN THE BLANKS

19. frosting
20. slow
21. rolled-out
22. poured fondant; simple or flat icing
23. glaze
24. royal icing
25. Italian buttercream
26. pastry cream-based buttercream
27. Italian/Swiss; Swiss/Italian
28. fudge/truffles; truffles/fudge
29. heavy cream
30. marzipan

TRUE OR FALSE

31. F
32. T
33. F
34. T
35. T
36. F
37. T
38. F
39. T
40. F

MULTIPLE CHOICE

41. A
42. C
43. B
44. A
45. A
46. C
47. C
48. A
49. B
50. B

MATCH THE FOLLOWING

51. I
52. C
53. J
54. D
55. F
56. E
57. H
58. A
59. G
60. B

Student Workbook Chapter 16

EXPLAIN THESE KEY TERMS

1. Bar cookie—A stiff dough formed into long, flattened, rectangular bars that are baked and then cut into slices
2. A diverse group of small sweet cakes or pastries described and categorized by how the dough is prepared and shaped for baking.
3. A mixing method where the sugar and fat are beaten until fluffy.
4. A soft moist cookie dough that is dropped from a spoon or ice cream scooper onto a sheet pan.
5. A cookie mixing method where eggs and sugar are beaten to a foam.
6. A category of cookie preparation where a stiff dough is rolled into small balls, flattened or crisscrossed with a fork, and then baked.
7. The easiest method for mixing cakes and cookies where all ingredients are placed in one bowl.
8. A category of cookie preparation in which the dough is pushed through a pastry bag into various shapes onto a sheet pan and baked.
9. A category of cookie preparation where a stiff dough is shaped into logs, wrapped well, and refrigerated or frozen until firm. The logs are then cut and baked.
10. A category of cookie preparation where a dough is refrigerated until firm and then rolled thin and cut into shapes before baking.
11. The category of cookie preparation where a batter is spread into a sheet pan with sides and baked. The sheet is then cut into squares or shapes.
12. The category of cookie preparation where a batter is spread onto a sheet pan or a stencil before being baked. Wafer cookies are soft when hot and harden as they cool.

FILL IN THE BLANKS

13. dough
14. piped cookies/wafer cookies; wafer cookies/piped cookies
15. dropped
16. refrigerator cookies
17. a sheet cookie
18. bar cookie
19. wafer cookie
20. piped cookie

TRUE OR FALSE

21. F
22. F
23. T
24. T
25. T
26. F
27. F
28. T
29. T
30. T

MULTIPLE CHOICE

31. B
32. A
33. A
34. C
35. C
36. A
37. B
38. A
39. B
40. B

MATCH THE FOLLOWING

41. D
42. B
43. A
44. I
45. J
46. C
47. H
48. F
49. E
50. G

Student Workbook Chapter 17

EXPLAIN THESE KEY TERMS

1. Sugar that is cooked to within the temperature interval of 320°–350°F which causes the sugar to develop a brown color and a rich intense flavor.
2. A test to determine whether a sugar syrup is done by dropping some syrup into a glass of cold water to see how easily it can be gathered into a ball.
3. The process by which particles of sugar form a repeated shape and are packed closely together to form crystals.
4. The method of preparing caramelized sugar by heating sugar in a heavy pan without water. An acid may be added.
5. Ingredients added to sugar syrup to prevent sugar molecules from re-crystallization by obstructing sugar molecules from joining together.
6. The process of preventing crystallization by adding an acid while heating a sugar syrup to break down the existing sugar into its component parts.
7. A sugar that is chemically different from sucrose used to control crystallization in a sugar solution.
8. A sugar syrup consisting of equal parts of water and granulated sugar, by weight, that is brought to a boil until the sugar is dissolved.
9. The substance that is dissolved in a solution.
10. The liquid that a substance is placed in to help it dissolve.
11. The chemical name for table or granulated sugar, derived from the sugar cane or sugar beet plant.
12. One or more sugars dissolved in water.
13. A method of preparing caramelized sugar by boiling a sugar syrup to the caramel stage.

FILL IN THE BLANKS

14. dissolved; brought to a boil
15. cooling
16. solutions
17. solvent/solute; solute/solvent
18. solute; solvent
19. heat; heat
20. evaporate
21. crystals

TRUE OR FALSE

22. F
23. T
24. F
25. F
26. T
27. T
28. T
29. F
30. F

MULTIPLE CHOICE

31. C
32. B
33. A
34. B
35. C
36. B
37. A
38. B
39. B
40. A

MATCH THE FOLLOWING

41. J
42. C
43. B
44. A
45. D
46. I
47. H
48. E
49. F
50. G

Student Workbook Chapter 18

EXPLAIN THESE KEY TERMS

1. A still frozen dessert that is made of layered, flavored mousses and molded.
2. One of two categories of frozen desserts that are churned or stirred as they freeze such as ice cream, sorbets and sherbets.
3. A sweetened, flavored, slushy ice that is scraped after freezing and scooped into glasses.
4. In frozen desserts a custard base lightened with meringue or whipped cream and still frozen.
5. A term used to describe how a food tastes and feels in the mouth.
6. The increase in volume due to the incorporation of air during the freezing process of ice cream and other churn frozen desserts.
7. An American parfait is made of layering ice creams with sauces, nuts and whipped cream. A European style parfait is a still frozen dessert made from a boiling sugar syrup beaten into egg yolks or whole eggs with whipped cream and flavors folded in.
8. A still frozen mousse or soufflé that in Italian means half frozen.
9. A churn frozen dessert usually fruit flavored that contains a small amount of milk or cream, and sometimes egg white or gelatin.
10. A churn frozen dessert that contains no diary products.
11. One of two categories of frozen desserts that lay still in the freezer with no agitation or churning as they freeze. This includes bombes, parfaits, mousses, and semifreddos.

FILL IN THE BLANKS

12. still
13. churned
14. pasteurized eggs
15. Gelato
16. sugar
17. 2%
18. Granita
19. fruit
20. whipped cream
21. Meringue

TRUE OR FALSE

22. T
23. F
24. T
25. F
26. F
27. F
28. T
29. T
30. F
31. T

MULTIPLE CHOICE

32. B
33. A
34. C
35. A
36. B
37. B
38. A
39. C
40. A
41. C

MATCH THE FOLLOWING

42. E
43. F
44. D
45. G
46. H
47. B
48. C
49. I
50. J
51. A

Student Workbook Chapter 19

EXPLAIN THESE KEY TERMS

1. Chocolate liquor in the solid state. Also referred to as unsweetened or bitter chocolate.
2. Semisweet chocolate contains less sugar than milk chocolate.
3. A whitish-gray spotty coating that appears on tempered chocolate that has been exposed to temperature variations and/or humidity.
4. The fruit of the Theobroma cacao tree from which chocolate derives.
5. A flavoring or product derived from the cocoa bean.
6. The dark liquidy paste created when chocolate nibs are crushed. When cooled into bricks or disks it is called unsweetened baking, or bitter chocolate.
7. The saturated fat that is naturally present in chocolate liquor that gives chocolate its characteristic velvety texture.
8. Chocolate that contains little or no cocoa butter and is used to coat candies.
9. High quality chocolate made with at least 32% cocoa butter that is used to make candy bars, in baked goods, or to coat candies and create decorations for all sorts of pastries. It comes in milk, semisweet, or white varieties.
10. Cocoa powder that has been treated with an alkali to neutralize its acidity.
11. A mixture of chocolate liquor cocoa butter, a minimum of 12% milk solids, sugar, and sometimes lecithin.
12. The powder formed by the separation of the cocoa butter from the chocolate liquor.
13. The material inside the hard outer shell of the cocoa bean. They are smashed and pulverized to form the chocolate liquor.
14. The result of chocolate being exposed to water or moisture when it thickens to a dried out, clumpy mass.
15. Bittersweet chocolate that contains less sugar than milk chocolate.
16. The stabilization of fat crystals within chocolate using a heating and cooling process.
17. A combination of cocoa butter milk solids, sugar, and flavorings but no actual chocolate.

FILL IN THE BLANKS

18. nibs; chocolate liquor
19. Cocoa butter
20. couverture; compound coating

TRUE OR FALSE

21. F
22. F
23. T
24. F
25. T
26. T
27. F
28. T
29. T
30. T

MULTIPLE CHOICE

31. A
32. B
33. B
34. C
35. C
36. B
37. A
38. C
39. A
40. A

MATCH THE FOLLOWING

41. C
42. E
43. B
44. J
45. F
46. D
47. G
48. H
49. I
50. A

Student Workbook Chapter 20

EXPLAIN THESE KEY TERMS

1. One of the basic sauce types it is made of cooked sugar with other ingredients or flavorings added.
2. An uncooked fruit sauce of fresh or frozen puréed fruit that is sweetened and strained.
3. A sweet French stirred custard sauce used as a dessert sauce or as a base for frozen desserts.
4. One of the six basic dessert sauces it is made of cooking egg yolks, sugar, some form of milk, and various flavorings.
5. A thickened liquid that is poured, drizzled, or piped onto a plate for decoration or directly on to the food.
6. The French or Italian name, respectively, for a type of custard sauce where eggs yolks are whisked with sugar or sugar syrup over a hot water bath until thickened.

FILL IN THE BLANKS

7. richness
8. custard/caramel; caramel/custard
9. uncooked fruit sauce
10. corn starch or arrowroot
11. smooth
12. edible

TRUE OR FALSE

13. T
14. F
15. T
16. F
17. T
18. F
19. T
20. T
21. F
22. T

MULTIPLE CHOICE

23. A
24. B
25. B
26. A
27. A
28. C
29. C
30. B

MATCH THE FOLLOWING

31. E
32. F
33. B
34. I
35. D
36. C
37. G
38. H
39. J
40. A

Student Workbook Chapter 21

EXPLAIN THESE KEY TERMS

1. Substitutes for sugar that are artificial or man-made in the laboratory.
2. Fats derived from animals with the exception of tropical plant oils and cocoa butter having a chemical structure where there are as many hydrogen atoms as possible bonded to the carbon atoms and all of the bonds are single.
3. Fats generally derived from plants that tend to be liquid at room temperature with the exception of partially hydrogenated vegetable shortenings.
4. Liquid fats, such as oils, that are partially hydrogenated to a solid or partially solid state at room temperature. The chemical structure of the fat is such that hydrogen atoms sit diagonally across the double bond. Trans-fats are associated with an increased risk of heart disease and certain cancers.

FILL IN THE BLANKS

5. refined
6. fiber
7. color
8. gluten
9. Fats
10. saturated
11. Trans-fats
12. sugar
13. sucrose
14. sucralose
15. sugar alcohols

TRUE OR FALSE

16. F
17. T
18. T
19. T
20. F
21. T
22. F
23. F
24. T
25. F
26. T
27. F
28. F
29. F
30. F

MULTIPLE CHOICE

31. B
32. A
33. C
34. A
35. C
36. B
37. B
38. A
39. B
40. A

MATCH THE FOLLOWING

41. E
42. C
43. I
44. J
45. F
46. D
47. H
48. G
49. B
50. A

Student Workbook Chapter 22

FILL IN THE BLANKS

1. oven thermometer
2. warm
3. curdle
4. plastic wrap; skin
5. too much
6. broke apart and crumbled
7. tough
8. over mixed
9. did not use
10. over beaten

TRUE OR FALSE

11. F
12. F
13. T
14. T
15. F
16. T
17. F
18. F
19. F
20. T

MULTIPLE CHOICE

21. A
22. C
23. C
24. B
25. B
26. A
27. B
28. A
29. C
30. A

MATCH THE FOLLOWING

31. H
32. C
33. J
34. I
35. E
36. F
37. A
38. B
39. D
40. G